TANKED
in
CINCINNATI

TANKED in CINCINNATI

Fortune & Calamity in the Beer Business

Michael D. Morgan
and Bret Kollmann Baker

AMERICAN PALATE

Published by American Palate
A Division of The History Press
Charleston, SC
www.historypress.com

Cover photo by Adam Rabinowitz.

First published 2024

Manufactured in the United States

ISBN 9781467157247

Library of Congress Control Number: 2024930892

Notice: The information in this book is true and complete to the best of our knowledge. It is offered without guarantee on the part of the authors or The History Press. The authors and The History Press disclaim all liability in connection with the use of this book.

Bret Kollmann Baker would like to dedicate his half of this book to his wife, Stephanie, for always supporting each other's dreams and hairbrained ideas without hesitation.

Michael D. Morgan would like to dedicate his half of this book to Jack, who recently stopped showing up behind the bar at Arnold's, and to Mike Bootes, who recently quit showing up on the other side of the same bar, which he did sometimes when he wasn't ripping up sidewalks with backhoes.

CONTENTS

PREFACE

In 2022, our acquisitions editor, John Rodrigue, tasked us with telling stories from the Cincinnati beer business. To his peril, he left that up to broad interpretation. We decided to approach the book interview-style rather than filtering other people's words and tone through our own. We sat down with the people in this book, drank beers and had conversations. *Tanked in Cincinnati* is composed of those sessions, with some narrative explanation in between. When we started lashing everything together, we quickly learned that word-for-word transcripts can be unreadable and often fail to capture the nuances of in-person conversations, especially after a few beers. So, all interviews have been edited for length and touched up lightly to allow the spoken word to translate to print. We have, however, done as little modification to exact words as possible with the intent of letting the personalities of everyone who has been part of this project come through these pages. We like, respect and have learned a lot from all these people, and if we've done our job properly, you will too.

ACKNOWLEDGEMENTS

We outlined everybody whom we wanted to interview for this book, then cut that number in half and eventually included about a third of that half. There are a lot more stories to tell, a lot of local pioneers who shaped the field. Thanks to all the people who helped transform the Greater Cincinnati brewing industry who aren't in this book but who would have been if we'd had the time and space. You know who you are.

Obviously, our greatest thanks go to the people who took the time out of their schedules to sit down in the *Brew Skies* studio to share their stories with us: Dave Heidrich, "Beer Dave" Gausepohl, Jim Koch, Dan Listermann, Scott LaFollette, Jim Tarbell, Mike "Jack" Toebbe (you are missed, friend), Lindsey Marie Bonadonna and Bryant Goulding. We also interviewed two generations of beer rep legends, Tom Jones and Matt Fiest. Due to space and some narrative complications, we were regrettably forced to cut that interview out, but it will make its way into another *Brew Skies* production by the time this book is released.

We'd also like to thank our wives. Bret's wife, Stephanie, and Mike's wife, Amy, put up with a lot of nonsense for the production of all things related to *Brew Skies*, and we couldn't do any of it without them. In addition to love, support and general tolerance of irresponsible behavior, they've both done a lot of proofreading to make this a better book.

On a weekly basis, our producers and directors, Dan Phenicie and Adam Rabinowitz, help make our various *Brew Skies* productions look and sound as good as they do. It may not be high art, but you can only work with what you've got.

Joanna, unfortunately we had to omit all of your dialogue. You were nonetheless vital to these interviews.

John Rodrigue, our acquisitions editor at The History Press, has been, as always, great to work with. Thank you. Maybe someday you'll finally come have a beer with us.

INTRODUCTION(S)

STARTING URBAN ARTIFACT

The founding of Urban Artifact happened rather quickly. Scotty and I had a business plan three years in the making, we had our life savings (lol) ready to spend, and we were now stuck waiting on the *exact right time* to start our brewery. It was June 2014 and my wife, Stephanie, had just got her master's degree. We decided to take a break from the grind and hike the Appalachian Trail, planning to be out for six months. Forty-one days into the trail, we get a call from a friend (Thanks, Matt!) about a possible lead on where to start our brewery. I called Scotty and filled him in on the situation. A friend of a friend, Scott Hand, posted on Facebook about starting a brewery. He had the location, he had the bank loan ready to go and, up until that very moment, he had a brewer partner and was desperate to find a replacement. Scotty wasted no time and started making calls, and in the meantime, Stephanie and I walked back into the woods, unreachable for four days.

Four days and forty-eight missed calls later, Scotty filled us in on the situation. Scott Hand was in a bind. His business partner lost all of his start-up money the day before they were set to close on their $1 million business loan. The bank gave Scott exactly two weeks to find both replacement capital and a replacement brewer. In a moment of sheer, life-altering luck, Scotty and I entered the scene perfectly prepared for this exact scenario. We had a business plan, we had the brewing acumen and, most importantly,

Working with this much fruit at a brewery can be dangerous. *Courtesy of Bret Kollmann Baker.*

we had the capital. After some quick phone calls to family, Stephanie and I were on a plane flying back to Cincinnati, closing on a business loan with Scotty and Scott. The ink dried and in a whirlwind of happenstance, Urban Artifact was born.

BRET KOLLMANN BAKER: FIGURE IT OUT

A mink farm is no place for farm-to-glass fermentation: mountains of excrement, viscera being ground into mink food, the burning stench of anal musk glands and, on certain days, the unholy aroma of burn-pit smoke.

But this unlikely setting, with the help of my friend Garrett, is *exactly* where I fell headfirst into alcoholic fermentation. The summer of 2005, as recent high school graduates, large portions of our week were tied up in figuring out how exactly to get ahold of beer for the weekend's events. It was on one particularly hot summer day when the obvious dawned on Garrett and me. Cider is an alcoholic drink. Cider comes from apples. Garrett has apple trees on his family's farm. We can figure this out. *We can make hard cider.*

Ten pounds of apples, a couple pounds of sugar, some cinnamon sticks for flavor, a packet of bread yeast and three weeks later, we had a party in a five-gallon bucket waiting for us in Garrett's farm basement. While I fondly remember these first sips of farm-fresh apple wine and my heart says it was some of the best booze I've ever had, my brain now knows it was probably hot liquid garbage. But that mattered little to us. We made a thing. We harnessed the power of *fungus* to make *alcohol.* We figured it out and imbued ourselves with the power of modern-day alchemy. I was hooked.

And the "hobby" progressed from there. I spent a couple years making (and eventually selling) wine from Walmart juice concentrates fermented in my college dorm closet (very illegal). This eventually turned into learning the process of homebrewing beer. Beer is how the next two most important and influential people on my fermentation journey came together: Scotty Hunter and Eric Heiden. Scotty and I would eventually become two-thirds of the Urban Artifact founding team. We started Ohio University's first homebrew club, the "Brew Crew" together. We brewed almost every weekend, attempting to figure out the science and mysticism behind fermenting beer. We even sold our plasma to make money to buy supplies at the local homebrew shop, the Athens DIY Shop, owned by Eric Hedin. Scotty and I would bring Eric our homebrews to share, and Eric would return the favor. We would chat process and technique every weekend, and over time Eric became a sponsor of the Brew Crew, helping us with brewing demos and events. Eric even helped us organize our infamous homebrew festival, featuring over twenty different kegs of homebrew all of which was subsequently shut down and raided by the Ohio Department of Liquor Control for "failure to pay excise taxes." No duh, ODLC. That is entirely the point of homebrewing. The point of all our undergraduate shenanigans is this: our curiosity around fermentation was far from sated.

Post graduation, Scotty and I entered the corporate grind. We worked, we saved money, and we spent our evenings scheming. Figuring out the business of beer was our shared passion. What, how, why? For the love of Bacchus, *why!?* Why should our shared dream of owning a brewery even exist? What gives us the right? And how on earth are we going to stand out from the crowd? The existential problem of starting our brewery took us three years to figure out, but we eventually landed on the driving business strategy that we still use to this day: "Get rich in your niche." We eventually settled on fruited and tart beer (*fruit tarts* as we lovingly call them), and the rest is Urban Artifact history.

Michael D. Morgan: My First Time

My first time wasn't good for anybody involved. As a kid, I collected beer cans. It was a common hobby back then in the early '80s, when I was a young nerd. Somewhere in the acquisition process, I wound up with a full can of generic beer. I'm not using the word *generic* to mean standard, yellow, American, mass-brewed beer. I'm telling you that it was literally generic. Briefly, that was a thing. It was either a white can with black block letters that simply said "BEER" or it was a Kroger version of the same concept, with Kroger's cost-cutter scissor logo above "BEER." I had both cans, and I forget which one was unopened, but it doesn't matter. I'm sure that both were terrible under optimal conditions, and "optimal conditions" is not how I drank my first beer. This perfect symbol of America's beer nadir had sat on a shelf in our basement for more than a year, maybe two, when at age fourteen my best friend, Raymond, and I stealthily snuck it out of the house, crouched down conspiratorially behind my family's backyard shed, cracked the pop top and prepared to become men. It was the '80s, and I knew from TV that there were two things that real men did. The first required girls, and I was failing miserably on that quest. The second was drinking beer, and commercials let me know that these two things went together. I didn't understand anything about women, but Bud Light ads suggested that the first step to attracting one was to drink the right beer.

Beer was about to be the answer to fixing everything wrong with my life at the time. It was a can full of infinite fun, a cure for social anxiety. It was the key to wooing the girl of my dreams (if I could get past her dad), and this transition in my life was about to start right now! Crouched facing each other, both of our heads swiveling a final time to scan for the prying eyes of adults, we steeled ourselves to commit our most serious crime to date, a perfect crime, the Leopold and Loeb of underage consumption. I brought the can to my lips and sipped it and then mustered all my nominal self-control to prevent my face from contorting when I assured Raymond, "It's not bad." Then it was his turn. Throughout junior high and high school, Raymond could be conspicuously emotive and blow our cover during nefarious activities, and this was the first time that I remember him losing his shit in a way that I thought was going to get us busted. He took a big swig and swallowed. His face scrunched up, and he began hopping and rolling around, loudly describing how this was the most disgusting thing he'd ever tasted. He was right, of course. I can't give you a full rundown of flavor notes decades later, but I still remember it being sour and vile. As aspiring men, however, we decided to finish it and at least experience getting drunk, but we didn't manage to get the whole thing down. Having each drank less than a full beer, we walked away proud that we'd lost our alcohol virginity, and we briefly convinced ourselves that we'd copped a buzz. But the truth was that my first experiment with beer was a failure that only taught me one thing: beer was disgusting.

I've had a comically unusual number of jobs and roles in life between that first beer and now, have been and become different people. Of my various and sundry talents and abilities, only one really seems to matter: resiliency. I can take a punch and keep getting up for another round—even when a smarter person would stay down. This tenacity was starting to take root in me when, a few months after that first beer, at age fifteen, I asked a guy whom I worked with in my grandparents' grocery store to buy a case of beer for Raymond and me. This time it was fresh, cold, premium beer—the best you could buy in Manchester, Ohio, in the mid-1980s: Michelob Light. It even came in a uniquely shaped bottle with a fancy label wrap that covered the cap. Ray's mom spent weekends with his grandmother, so we had a safe place to hunker down for this fateful Saturday night. We even invited some girls over, although they didn't show up. I don't know how much of that case we drank, but we didn't have to convince ourselves that we were drunk this time. We got tanked. Beer, however, still sucked. It was too big of a leap from the sugary sodas that I'd grown up drinking. It was bitter, but getting wasted rocked. It was, as we said at the time, rad to the max, but there had to be a better way to get there than beer. Fortunately, two old guys on TV commercials named Bartles and James came to the rescue and improved the trip to getting hella wasted the next weekend and several that followed.

When I was invited to go cruising with two much cooler, slightly older guys a few weeks later, Ernie, the driver, asked what I wanted to drink as he rolled up to the carryout window. Kevin swiveled in the passenger seat and stuck his open palm into the back for my money. I handed Kevin money, and

I confidently answered Ernie as an experienced drinker: "Bartles & James orange wine coolers." Ernie ordered a case of Miller Genuine Draft, paid for it and drove away as I sat befuddled. When I say that these guys were "older," I mean sixteen, maybe seventeen—older than me and licensed to drive, but still minors. It was a lot easier for kids to buy booze in the '80s, but it was still as illegal as it is today, so I waited to ask what had happened to my wine coolers. "Girls drink that," he said, and Kevin very helpfully added, "You aren't a pussy are you?" "No." It was, of course, the only real answer to the question. Kevin tossed me a can of MGD, and I choked half of it down and threw the rest out the window—where the empties went—when the next one came flying into the backseat toward me. By the end of the night, I was keeping pace. I learned two important things that night: real men drank beer, and no matter how much something cost, Kevin would never voluntarily give you change back.

By sixteen, I'd mostly traded the nerd image in for a Spuds Mackenzie–inspired party animal with low-grade criminal tendencies. I did well in school, and my loving mother made sure that I dressed like a proper '80s preppy. But by applying my natural leadership skills to bodacious backroad parties and organized chaos, my reputation grew legendarily bad. Beer didn't cause the girl of my dreams to fall in love with me, but it dramatically improved my social status.

Around my senior year, I discovered Herman Joseph. The brand dates back to the 1850s, and it has had several iterations since then. In the late '80s, it was what we would call a "crafty" beer today, a brand created by a large, national or international brewery to compete in the craft beer market. I don't remember what it tasted like, but it was the first time that I started to veer toward something different, more flavorful, as miniscule as the difference probably was. A few years after I started drinking beer—a lot of it—I started actually enjoying it, drinking it partly for how it tasted versus as a means to an end. In college, craft beer was the most acceptable drug that I experimented with, but it wasn't at the top of the list because it cost so much more than Natural Light (and didn't last as long as mushrooms). It wasn't until I got a bartending job at a craft brewery called Oldenberg in the mid-'90s that I took the first next step in appreciating good beer, but we'll get back to that later.

My early beer journey had been two-pronged. In my twenties, I learned to appreciate beer, but that only happened after I had developed an unhealthy relationship with it in my teens. In this way, my own beer story in the 1980s and '90s mirrored America's relationship with beer. There

Mike at age fifteen, sporting a Spuds Mackenzie T-shirt and a bad attitude. *Courtesy of Cynda Morgan.*

were two very different forces at work shaping that national relationship. National beer companies like Anheuser-Busch were tailoring ad campaigns to "contemporary adults," also known as "heavy users" when I was in high school. These were euphemisms for binge drinkers between twenty-one and twenty-four years old, but in reality, some observers believed that Bud Light's Spuds Mackenzie ad campaign—featuring a bull terrier as "the original party animal"—was aimed at building brand loyalty in people under twenty-one. Organizations like MADD and the National Parent Teacher Association accused Anheuser-Busch of targeting minors, teenagers—me!—with ads that pushed toxic masculinity and subtly promoted binge drinking. At the same time, the first craft breweries were starting to elevate beer as a complex, flavorful drink to be sipped, savored and enjoyed.

In 1981, Americans drank more beer per capita than any other year in the post-Prohibition world, and this stat was driven by record sales of bad, watery, rice- and corn-spiked light beer. I didn't get started on my personal path to mass consumption of terrible beer until a few years later. Eventually, like Gen X America as a whole, I slowly started to explore craft beers—or "microbrews," as they used to be known—but it was a slow, gradual transition. I continued to pound the hell out of hackneyed yellow beer well past the age when an adult should stop being proud of how fast he can shotgun a Busch Light. I'm confessing this for a reason. What inspired Bret and I to write this book was not a feel-good story about how everything about beer and the beer industry is good and happy and makes the world a better place. Like our podcast, *Brew Skies Happy Hour*, we're interested in the deeper story, the broader social factors that help determine what and how different generations drink. Does the industry drive the consumer or vice versa? We also want to tell the true stories from the perspective of the people who have lived and breathed the beer business, the local pioneers and the successful inspirations and, more importantly, to look for wisdom from the people who were on the cusp of boundless riches when the wheels came off. Along the way, Bret and I will also share some of our own stories of how we became so deeply engrained in the business of beer. Crack open whatever you like to drink and let's get started.

OLDENBERG

How Dave Heidrich Changed the World, but Why He Doesn't Own a Yacht

MIKE: In the mid-'90s, I got a bartending job at Oldenberg. I started tending bar in college because bartending was the only thing that my psychology degree qualified me to do, and it didn't really qualify me to do that. I'd spent my bartending time serving Bud Lights, Sex on the Beach and Flaming Dr Peppers. I didn't know anything about beer. Oldenberg was doing more than making great beer—they were also proselytizing, actively spreading knowledge, educating their consumer base, which started with educating their bartenders and servers. Before I ever poured a beer, I had to attend a training session where we drank beer and learned the basics of different styles. At the time, it was the best day of work in my life. We tasted an aged Belgian ale made with wild yeast. Learning that the flavor of the beer was connected to random funk floating around in the air blew my mind. I had drunk and enjoyed some craft and imported beers by then, but I didn't know enough to understand why I did or didn't like different styles. Oldenberg is largely responsible for turning me on to good beer.

In 1982, California became the first state to legalize brewpubs, enabling the first modern microbreweries to sell directly to consumers as opposed to selling wholesale to bars. Direct-to-consumer sales constitutes most of the profit made from a glass of beer, so this was a sea change. It made it possible for small-scale brewing to be profitable. In 1983, Mendocino Brewing Company became the first legal brewpub in the U.S., followed a month later by Buffalo Bill's Brewery in Hayward, California, opened by a very colorful photojournalist and homebrew book author named Bill Owens.

When Dave Heidrich and his father-in-law opened Oldenberg Brewery in September 1987 in Fort Mitchell, Kentucky, roughly six miles south of downtown Cincinnati, they were at the forefront of a national movement. They also designed and operated Oldenberg in ways that were unprecedented—and they made great beer! Oldenberg did everything right: its Beer Camp drew international attendees, its beer was hailed and when Heidrich and his partners decided to open multiple locations in different states, investors flocked to fund it. Oldenberg was on the cusp of becoming the first great national brewpub chain, and Heidrich was poised to become a billionaire. Then the wheels fell off. We ask Dave, "WTF?!"

DAVE: It was March of 1983, and there was an article in the center column of the *Wall Street Journal* that talked about Buffalo Bill Owens. He was out getting a license to sell his homebrew, which was a pretty rare phenomenon. About a week later, I think the Wiedemann brewery in Newport announced that it was closing, and it was the last functioning brewery in the state of Kentucky. So, I thought that might be a cool little thing to do. I had no background or experience in making beer. I mentioned it to my father-in-law one day, and he looked at me and he goes, "Yeah, let's do that." We would build a beer hall, and we could perform the *Flying Dutchman* opera in there. So, off we went to try to figure it out. It's hard to believe, but in those days, if you wanted to learn about something, you went to the library—and that's how we got started.

I think it was a couple of months later that I found out that the American Homebrewers Association was having their annual meeting in Boulder. For the first time ever, they were going to have kind of a sidetrack about guys starting microbreweries. So, I flew to Boulder. At this time, I was practicing law for a living, and I go to this homebrew meeting wearing what I wore to work every day: a coat and tie. Only one other guy showed up with a tie on, and that was Jim Koch (founder of Boston Beer Company, creator of Sam Adams). He was working for Boston Consulting Group. He walks over to me and says, "Dude, we're a bit out of place here." We were great friends for many years. I came back full of a lot of knowledge, and we started knocking down hurdles to building a brewery—like making it legal in the state of Kentucky to build a brewery and restaurant. Nobody was building small breweries. When I was trying to figure out who could build it, I went to a brewery in Little Rock. This guy was convinced that he knew how to build our brewery. I went there, and everything was kind of jury-rigged. I went into the bathroom at this brewery and the urinal is hanging

A twentysomething Dave Heidrich posing with part of the new brew system at Oldenberg. *Courtesy of Dave Heidrich.*

on the wall. I'm six-four—I'm a tall guy. But they had an old Coke bottle case on the floor that I had to stand on so that I could reach the urinal. I thought, if this dude does not know how high to hang a urinal, he can't build our brewery. He got disqualified. That is not germane to the story, but it just came back to me.

MIKE: But it is germane in the sense that a lot of those early breweries were guys putting things together out of spare parts. And that's not what you guys did. You built a world-class facility.

DAVE: We found out that, lo and behold, one of the great American brewery builders was right here in Cincinnati. At the time they were called Bishoprick, now known as EnerFab. And they were building for everybody. There was not a major brewery in America that didn't have Bishoprick tanks in it. I told them what we wanted to do, and thankfully they were going through a lot of changes. Their sales manager said, "We're gonna have to learn about these small breweries because the big breweries aren't building anymore, and if we're gonna stay in business, we're gonna have to figure this out." I don't know that they made any money on building our brewery, but I had the benefit of an awful lot of expertise that a lot of my cohorts at that time didn't.

BRET: That's an amazing, amazing coincidence that they just happened to be five miles from where you guys were building your brewery, with that level of expertise, looking to transition into the craft industry, because they were also seeing the changes, and it sounds like they cut you a great deal.

DAVE: Yeah, they did. Well, I assume they did. It was hard to price shop anything in those days. They had trouble scaling down their thinking—they were used to building storage tanks that would handle six hundred barrels, and I was building a twenty-five-barrel brewhouse with fifty-barrel storage tanks. That was the smallest thing they'd ever done, but there was an awful lot of knowledge about brewhouse design that, unless you went to Europe, you couldn't find in the U.S. at the time.

MIKE: You start out with this fantastic brewhouse, and the larger brewery itself was also really impressive.

DAVE: My father-in-law owned the Drawbridge Inn, which was a very successful hotel in Fort Mitchell, Kentucky. So, he was doing well. He was a guy that has a gift for hospitality, and he was a custom home builder by training. So, we got to fulfill an awful lot of his dreams in building a classic-looking brick brewery like you would have built in Over-the-Rhine in 1870. There was an awful lot of masonry, fancy corbels. The beer hall held about seven hundred people. We had a separate pub up top that was called JD Brews at the time, which was a couple-hundred-seat restaurant.

Then, an attorney calls me from Wisconsin, and he says, "I represent the folks that have the largest collection of breweriana in the world." I didn't know what breweriana was. The collection was fifty thousand cans strong and tens of thousands of trays and signs and anything that had a beer name on it in the United States. We were able to make a deal with them, and we covered the walls with all of this history.

BRET: How was that build-out? Everything was brick and built to look historic. That couldn't have been cheap or easy.

DAVE: You're correct on both counts. The entire project ended up costing $7 million, which in 1987 dollars is a lot of money. About a million of that was brewing equipment, including the bottling line. The rest of it was all building.

BRET: I read that your brewery had the capacity for twenty-five thousand barrels, which is a shitload of beer, especially in 1986. Did you guys open with that capacity?

DAVE: Ultimately, what affects your capacity is what your storage capacity is and how long you're going to store your product. We started out making lagers, and it was a thirty- to thirty-two-day lagering process, and I had 1,200 barrels of fermentation capacity. So, if you can only turn that over every thirty-one days, you're only going to get 15,000 barrels out of it.

MIKE: I've read that you brought your brewer from Germany?

DAVE: He was actually in L.A. when I found him, but he's originally from Germany. His name is Hans Bilger. He was working for the Pabst Brewing Company in L.A. We moved him here, and he was great. The dude was

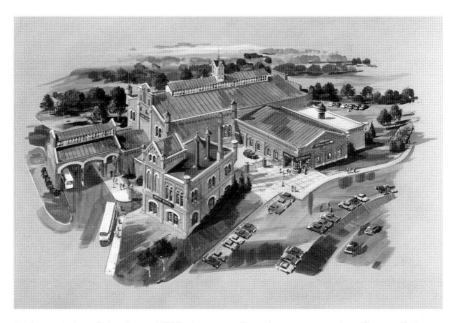

Artist rendering of the planned Oldenberg complex prior to construction. *Courtesy of the Kenton County Public Library, Covington, Kentucky.*

a graduate of Weihenstephaner, had his degree in brewing, and that was hard to find. The local talent were working at Hudepohl-Schoenling or Wiedemann, but by that point they'd been out of brewery work for three or four years, so they'd all gone off to do something else and most of those guys kind of learned the business in the plant that they were in. They were great at what they did, but we were starting from scratch. So, having a guy that was classically trained really served us well.

BRET: What were your bestsellers? Did you try to chase customer trends to a degree, or was it like, "We're going to make the best pilsner that we can, and we know people are going to buy it?"

DAVE: Uhm, not the latter. We set out to make a beer that had more body and more flavor than what the classic American light lagers had. Christian Moerlein had been in the market and had woken some people up to a little more flavor. We were making great beers, but they were designed to appeal to the consumer base at the time. A guy didn't say, "I like this versus that"; his question was, "Do I like that versus Michelob?" Do you like that versus Bud Light? That's all they had to compare to. It was the pioneer days.

MIKE: You didn't start by going over the consumer's head. You were moving the consumer up from what they were used to, but they were still lighter-bodied golden lagers and pilsners. I think that was a really smart move. In the beer class that I teach, I always refer to good pilsners or golden lagers as "gateway drugs." They're a nice first step into the world of good beer.

DAVE: Yeah, there were guys in the late '80s on the West Coast that we're making a bit more flavorful beers, but that was the West Coast. It was Northern California and Portland, some in Seattle. Then, of course, Jim Koch came out with Sam Adams, which was considered for years and years to be a big, bold, massive leap of trust when a consumer bought that heavy beer. We had to deal with what we had to deal with.

BRET: Things were changing rapidly in the '90s. Craft beer was gaining a little bit of more steam. Big beer was getting into it and trying to obfuscate what was craft beer or not craft beer. Eventually you started getting price wars for some of these bigger craft breweries that were distributing. Things started getting really wild in the '90s. Did you guys find that you were initially a little more insulated from all that by being in Cincinnati?

Hans Bilger, Oldenberg's German brewmaster. *Courtesy of the Kenton County Public Library, Covington, Kentucky.*

DAVE: Well, insulated, yes, but I think Cincinnati could have benefited from additional production. We were out there having to carry the load on our own. The problem was, I didn't have anybody else out here evangelizing for more flavorful beer. There was Barrel House Brewing, but they only distributed a little bit. I contract-brewed for a guy in town that had a beer called Mad Monk. Everybody asked, "Why are you doing that?" I'd say, "Well, I've got capacity, and he's going to have three of his own people out there every day, telling consumers that they should explore more beer." Cincinnati was slow to the party.

MIKE: You guys were also doing a beer camp, a multi-day experience where people would come and drink a lot of beer and learn things. It sounds like a lot of fun, but it was more than that. You were training your consumers as well.

DAVE: That was a heck of a lot of fun, and that event got a lot of notoriety. We would bring about three hundred people in for the weekend. They would come on Friday afternoon, and Friday evening we would do a little opening session. We would get as much beer in as we could from all over the country—both imports and domestics, craft beer, big brewer beer. We just tried to have the biggest selection of beer anybody had ever seen, and the Bloatarians, the local homebrew club, would come and volunteer and man the bar. Those guys and gals know an awful lot about beer, so they helped educate. We spent the better part of Saturday with a group of speakers— Greg Smith, who's an author of a lot of beer books; Michael Jackson from London came; Kim Jordan from New Belgium; Pete Slosberg (of Pete's Wicked Ale); Jeff from Left Hand brewing in Denver. These guys would come in and spend the weekend with people, and it was great. People got a chance to spend time in the brewery if they wanted to go through making a batch of beer, starting at the beginning. The Bloatarians would do a homebrewing session. We'd do a big dinner on Saturday night, seven courses, and there was beer in each one of the courses, and then it was served with another beer that complemented it.

BRET: You started that in 1992, and earlier today I read an article from the *Chicago Tribune*, from 1997. It was after beer camp five. You were making national news with this beer camp. They were quoting you in it, and I really wish I could have heard some of your, quote, "vented righteous anger" from back then.

DAVE: The London newspaper sent a guy from London to cover beer camp, and they wrote about it, but it was the '90s and people were starting to get interested in beer and so the public wanted to know and the press wanted to cover it—plus, let's face it, if you're a journalist and you read about this, you're going to go to your boss and say, "Hey, Mr. Editor, why don't you cover me for a weekend to go drink beer for a living?"

BRET: Everything about it sounds wonderful, and the fact that you pioneered that? I mean, Sierra Nevada still does the beer camp idea. They started doing it around twenty years after you guys first did it.

DAVE: Yeah, yeah, they're good guys.

MIKE: Here's what I don't understand about Oldenberg, Dave. Bret started out by saying this is a fantastic story, and it is up until the point where it seems to become a shitty story.

DAVE: Yeah, that's a good description. It did not end well.

MIKE: There is some of the history that I remember personally, but I did go back and read some things, and it strikes me that what you guys were doing in the late '80s, especially for this part of the country, was revolutionary. The beer camp idea is incredibly inventive. You had a world-class facility, you had a world-class brewer, you were making award-winning beers, you were starting to expand into other locations. Everything about it looked like you were waking up every day and knocking it out of the park, but somewhere in the late '90s, the wheels started to come off. What happened?

DAVE: We started brewing in '87, and I ended up buying the brewery from my father-in-law in the early '90s. We raised some money, we did a little stock offering, we sold a lot of stock to individuals in Cincinnati. We raised some money from bigger investors, but then we followed what was a bit of a trend at the time. We had a wide variety of shareholders that couldn't buy in at $500. So, we were trying to enlist our own consumers. You could say you were an owner of the brewery.

BRET: Sam Adams used that technique as well.

DAVE: Yes, I know. I'm a business guy first. I'm a lawyer. I'm a finance major, so I'm always trying to look at the business model, and quite frankly, while we were doing really well compared to other midwestern brewers, there was not a big exit strategy for the beer business. We were going to be a $2 million-a-year brewery. That's where I could see us getting, and that didn't have a whole lot of easy ways to monetize the investment for the people that invested. The guys that put five hundred bucks in, they were happy to come to the shareholder parties, but for other people, you need to find a way that you can return their investment. In business school, they always ask, "What are the barriers to entry?" Well, the barriers to entry are sometimes less than the barriers to exit when you build a very capital-intensive business and you owe the bank a lot of money and you owe your shareholders money. How do I monetize this? To me, it made sense to develop additional restaurant assets. When we raised money, the game plan was, we were going to grow some more restaurants where we would brew beer, and that would be an extension of the brand name. Besides the original brewery, we opened the Holy Grail in Clifton. We were able to buy a place in Lexington that had started as a brewery and lasted like ninety days for some reason. I forget what the guy's problem was, but we bought a place in Lexington. We were approached by some guys in Louisville that wanted to do a higher-end concept. At that time, there were maybe four Rock Bottom breweries in the country, and they seemed to have a different model that was much more akin a scalable restaurant. The Holy Grail in Clifton was a great college bar, but it was not going to be something that you could build a dozen of without a whole lot of unique things lining up. These guys in Louisville had a lot of experience. They had been involved in building restaurant chains like Texas Roadhouse, Chi-Chis, Tumbleweed and a couple others, and they had an idea. So, we hitched our wagon with them. We built the Oldenberg Grill in Louisville, which was a much bigger place than the Holy Grail—more along the lines of what you may have seen at Rock Bottom. And we replicated that in Augusta, Georgia, and in Orlando, Florida. And we had other sites already identified that we owned in Fort Wayne, one in New Jersey, one in Buffalo. We were on a tear.

Then, quite frankly, my partners had some issues with some of their other businesses, and the wheels came off quickly. If you are a fast-growing enterprise and you're in the restaurant business, you better know what you're doing, and I grew a little too big for my britches is what my mother would say. We went from one location in Fort Mitchell to five locations and six hundred employees, and we did not have the controls and the processes in place. So, I had to unravel that, you know? There was no ability to make that work. We had some bad deals on some leases and the like. In the end, I had to sell most of that off. We sold the original brewery. The restaurants were all one-off deals. The brewery in Fort Mitchell was sold to some guys out of Indiana that had just—this is 1999, the first dot-com bubble—and these guys had written some code for something, I forget what it was. They were very young like twenty-nine, thirty years old, and somebody had given them $12 or $15 million for this piece of code they wrote, so they thought it'd be fun to own a brewery, and I needed somebody else to own a brewery.

They bought it. They ran it for about a year and a half. I left, but a lot of my employees that were running the brewery stayed, obviously. I still remember my marketing person calling me about four months after I'd sold the brewery. He said, "Guess what? We've got a suite at the Kentucky Speedway." I go, "Okay, well, that's an interesting investment of money." And he says, "Heidrich, when you were here, if I gave a guy a T-shirt, he had to promise us a tap knob, and they had to name a child after us if they were going to get a neon sign." He says, "These guys have custom-made golf bags that say 'Oldenberg Beer' embroidered on them." I just said, "Gosh, maybe that was a mistake, maybe it's why I didn't make it in the business." After about eighteen months, their accountants got ahold of them and said,

"You guys are very wealthy, and you're going to be very unwealthy if you continue this," so they sold it off at that point. That's when they stopped making the beer. They sold the brewing equipment to AllTech. It was an unglamorous finish.

A friend of mine, Daniel Bradford, is with the American Homebrewers, and he ran the Brewers Association of America, and he owned All About Beer magazine for many years. Daniel and I still talk, and he called me a couple years ago said, "I'm cleaning out some crap in my basement, and I found the minutes of the Small Brewers Association of America, the Board of Directors Minutes from 1994." I said, "Those were great days." He goes, "Yeah, you were chairman in '94, '95." I said, "Oh yeah, I was." Then he read me the list of the people that were on the board then. It included Jim Koch, billionaire; Kenny Grossman from Sierra, billionaire; Kim Jordan; Jack Joyce from Rogue Ales; guy from up in Boston; and four or five other names of people that have all made fortunes in the business. Then there's three or four names on that list, like mine, that if you weren't in Cincinnati, you'd have never heard of. Some pioneers die on the trail. It's okay.

MIKE: How much of it had to do with unique internal things as opposed to what was going on in the industry more broadly in the '90s?

DAVE: Me exiting the beer business had to do with a too aggressive growth strategy for restaurants, too much too quick. The lesson that I've learned over the years is just because someone's willing to invest in you is not necessarily validation that you've got it figured out or that your business plan will work. It just means that somebody believes it will. I was able to attract a lot of capital, and I thought, damn, these guys are wealthy, and they've made a lot of money, and they're telling me, "Here's another half million dollars, go open up another restaurant," so I guess I should do that—and that was ill-advised. I just grew too quick, too fast. Now, the reason that I think that the brand and Oldenberg failed overall is because it was Cincinnati, and we were not Portland or Denver or Seattle, even; in 2001, there was no craft beer culture to speak of.

BRET: No, it took a long time for Cincinnati to catch up. We have a lot of breweries now, but you were well ahead of the game.

DAVE: Yeah, it was fun.

MIKE: It's frustrating how close you were to riding a huge wave. There was just a few years difference between being too far ahead of your time to be sustainable and to the period when craft beer exploded nationally. If Oldenberg had still been functioning in 2010…

DAVE: I think I'd be talking to you from my boat in the Caribbean. It must've been twenty years now, stepping out of business, which is hard to believe, but those lessons are hard to learn in life. I've gone into commercial real estate development, and the lessons of a business failure—if you use them right—can be very valuable. Almost every city had its Oldenberg. The early adopter doesn't always win.

BRET: That's a pretty well proven. Just because you're first doesn't mean you're the one who's going to benefit from the foundation you lay. Usually, somebody else comes in, or the market finally comes around, and then things get built on the backs of those who did the hard work.

MIKE: One of my favorite quotes is, "The pioneers get the arrows and the settlers get the land."

DAVE: Oh, there you go.

BRET: As someone who lived through the boom-bust of the '90s with craft beer, do you see something similar happening today?

DAVE: I don't know because I don't know the economics of the business the way I did then. I think that it's going to be hard for a metropolitan area the size of Cincinnati, just a couple of million people, to support more than two or three major production beer brands. The ability to support your business through a taproom is great. Again, I'm a business school guy, so I'm always asking, "What's the exit? Who is going to pay me, and how much will they pay me for this business at any given time?" A lot of people are in the business because it's a labor of love. But man, I see more and more bigger and more expensive facilities going up, and I hope it works. In many ways, most of these are just a restaurant business, and how many independent restaurants do you know? You know some, right? How many of them have successively sold to a new owner that is not the founder? They are a very, very tough thing to sell. An awful lot of great guys become restaurateurs, and then they get to a point when they realize that unless one of their kids is going to take it over, they don't have a plan. They rarely sell it for a nice fat check and walk away. There are only three exit strategies for an independent restaurant: bankruptcy, arson and suicide.

BRET: Oh God! That's dark!

DAVE: It is dark, but go out and prove me wrong.

MIKE: Look for Dave's column in *Restaurant Weekly*, next week.

DAVE: I've been an entrepreneur; I've been in all kinds of businesses and still am. Starting an independent restaurant and then exiting that business is tough. I thought I had to grow to twelve restaurants—twelve was kind of my magic number. I thought that was the next level of valuation and financing, but I never got there. I burned up before I got there. It's hard to think about an exit. So, that's a long answer to what's going to happen in the beer business, but that's what I think of when I see a new brewpub opening up—a couple-million-dollar investment—every three weeks.

BRET: That's where my head's at too. Neighborhood breweries are mimicking the restaurant industry a lot. I think that you can stay small and

Oldenberg Brewery, Fort Mitchell, Kentucky, in postcard form. *Courtesy of Dave Heidrich.*

be able to pay yourself enough money that you're going to be a successful business owner who can retire comfortably, but the idea that you're going to get rich is almost never going to happen. You can only have so many regional production breweries. It's going to be interesting to see how this shakes out. That was extremely insightful, Dave. Thank you for the conversation.

DAVE: No, thank you.

MIKE: I also want to say thanks for everything that you did for beer culture here. It's not a story with a happy ending, but along the way, you trained a lot of people to drink better beer and you lit a spark that helped feed the long-term success of craft. You also helped a lot of people like me grow our palates. In the short time that I worked for Oldenberg, you gave me a real appreciation for beer. I'm sorry you're not a billionaire.

DAVE: Hey, so is my wife.

◆ ◆ ◆

Today, the $7 million investment made to build the Oldenberg brewery in 1987 would be roughly equivalent to $18 million. It was fifty thousand square feet, thirty thousand of which was composed of the awe-inspiring grand hall. The building was sold to Jerry Carroll in 2001, a developer and owner of the Kentucky Speedway. In April of that year, Oldenberg brewed its last batch of beer. Carroll announced a lot of plans for the building that included a NASCAR-themed restaurant, a casino, and a $2 million to $3 million conversion to mixed-use development in 2007. None of it materialized, but through his different plans and visions, Carroll always showed a great respect for the work and craftsmanship that went into the building, a rare piece of construction from the 1980s that retained its beauty and relevance over time. Neyer Construction, however, is not known for its appreciation of aesthetics, so it promptly began demolishing the building after purchasing it in 2013. The following year, it also demolished the 382-room Drawbridge Inn. It replaced these iconic scenes of local beer legend with a medical office building and some heinous strip mall retail.

BEER DAVE

The Birth and Rise of a Legend

Dave Gausepohl was one of the first employees of Oldenberg Brewery when it opened. He held a variety of positions there, including a pivotal role in organizing Beer Camp. In 1994, Ken Lewis, a visionary entrepreneur in the alcoholic beverage industry, opened Party Source, a Northern Kentucky liquor store built on a nationally unprecedented scale. Lewis transformed the experience of buying liquor, beer and wine with an astounding selection and a knowledgeable staff. Dave took the knowledge and contacts of the nascent craft beer industry to Party Source, becoming the nation's first beer curator, building and overseeing the best selection of beer under one roof in the United States. Along the way, he became "Beer Dave," the go-to expert on beer for local media outlets. The moniker, his knowledge and his sense of humor made Beer Dave a local celebrity. These days, he has a weekly segment on the Mike McConnell show, a popular, long-running talk show on AM radio station 700 WLW.

❖ ❖ ❖

BRET: We've heard that, given your age at the time, Oldenberg was probably your first job in beer?

DAVE: Right. I crashed the groundbreaking ceremony at Oldenberg to get the job. I was like, "Okay, there's going to be a brewery opening up in the county that I was born in," and I'm like, "How can I not do this?" So, I showed up as this pie-eyed little kid like, "I'm going to work here and stuff," and the guy's like, "Go away, kid, you bother me and stuff." I was like, "No, no, I'm going to work in your brewery." He tells me that it's going to be at least a year before the thing opens. I said, "That's why I'm here, to find out who I need to talk to to work at the Drawbridge until the brewery opens. Then I want to work in the brewery." Within a week, I was waiting tables at the Drawbridge, and within nine months, they gave me wind that they were going to do the first brew. I showed up as an unpaid, pie-eyed kid again to watch the first brew. At 4:30 in the morning, we finally got it into the fermenting tanks, and that's a long day. I went home, and I got called the next day by Hans Bilger, the brewmaster. He said, "I cannot have you not be in this brewery. You've shown all kinds of enthusiasm, and you absolutely need to be part of this." I'd just turned twenty-one, and the rest is history.

MIKE: What role did this pie-eyed kid serve at Oldenberg?

DAVE: I started as a brewer, and they quickly had me on all kinds of other things. By the end, I was running all their beer camps and doing a lot of special events. I was writing their quarterly newsletter and just anything that needed to happen. By just crashing a groundbreaking ceremony, it got me that far. It was pretty obvious that beer was going to be what I was going to spend the rest of my life at. People always ask, "How did you know that you were going to spend all this time in beer in the fourth grade, when I started collecting beer cans?" I realized that I'm going to need a job. I'm going to get a car payment, a house payment, all this kind of stuff. Why not work in the beer business? So, since the fourth grade, that's what I wanted to do.

BRET: Is that when you got the nickname "Beer Dave," in fourth grade?

DAVE: No. The nickname came on Halloween 1995, my first full day at the Party Source. The office manager pulled me and David, the specialty wine buyer, over, and she says, "One of you has to have a nickname." David says, "Well, I was here first." She's like, "Neither one of you cares if you're Dave or David, so we need a nickname for one of you." I said, "All right, do you have a suggestion?" And she said, "We've been calling you 'Dave the beer guy,' but that won't fit on a name tag. What if we call you 'Beer Dave'? That'll fit on your name tag." Three days later, I had a Party Source Beer Dave name tag, and about a month later, I was doing some

The Grand Hall at Oldenberg Brewery, showing thirty thousand square feet of serving space and the world's largest breweriana museum. *Courtesy of Dave Heidrich.*

radio commercials saying, "Come see Beer Dave and the world's largest selection of beer." The rest is this history.

BRET: There's a thing with nicknames. If you go onto the playground as a kid and you tell your friends, "I've got a new name. I want you guys to start calling me this," you'll get a nickname that day, but it won't be the one you want.

DAVE: Yeah, I won the lottery on nicknames. I have to agree with that, but it's funny—there are people who don't even know my last name.

MIKE: Is it true that you were really the very first craft beer buyer in the U.S.?

DAVE: Yeah. I met with Ken Lewis [the founder and then-owner of Party Source], and he said, "Nobody else is doing this. I've watched what has happened with wine, and we're going to strike while the iron is hot and do it with beer." Nowadays, there's craft beer buyers at gas stations, but somebody needed to be that guy, and I said, "I'll be the guy."

MIKE: What made you the guy to be the first craft beer buyer in the country at the time? Was it from managing the beer camps at Oldenberg?

DAVE: Those were epic. Yeah, when I was doing the beer camps, that's where I was making all the connections with the various breweries and importers. I was lining up internationally known speakers, and we were bringing in beers like Samuel Smith's, Lindemann's, Trappist, and nobody knew what these things were. That gave me a good résumé. I was also studying it like other guys know baseball scores. That was my knowledge—beer—and so, you know, and that's what they needed. If I cut myself in the store, it was going to foam.

MIKE: Did you get to hang out with a lot of the really early people?

DAVE: Yeah. Jim Koch [of Sam Adams] and Ken Grossman [of Sierra Nevada], Pete Slosberg [of Pete's Wicked Ale]. Some of them are still on my cellphone today.

BRET: Is that where Sierra Nevada got their beer camp idea from?

DAVE: They didn't get it from me, but I think that it was part of the intellectual property of Oldenberg, and the last guy that owned the rights didn't pay the lawyer fees to keep the trademark alive, and Sierra Nevada either got it that way or that guy sold it to Sierra Nevada. But yes, there's absolutely a connection.

MIKE: Do you have any favorite stories from beer camp? Like somebody that's a billionaire today getting really hammered and pissing in a plant or something?

DAVE: The one I'll always remember was two weeks before one of the beer camps, it was announced that Miller was going to pull the plug on Miller Clear…

MIKE: What the hell was that?!

DAVE: They were not going to make clear beer anymore. Zima came out and was selling really well, so Miller was like, "Well, that's it." People don't like color in their beer, so they literally made a beer that had no color. It tasted like beer. Well, Miller beer. Then they announced that they were going to pull the plug on it, so we built a coffin, and we had a funeral for Miller Clear beer. We put a six-pack of Miller Clear in the coffin. We had a deacon or something come and perform a little ceremony with last rights, and we put the top on the casket. Before you could get in line to go to dinner, you had to take this pneumatic nail gun and drive a nail into the coffin. So, everyone that was at beer camp that year got to drive one of the final nails in the coffin for Miller Clear beer.

MIKE: I tended bar briefly at Oldenberg's location at the airport. As part of the job, I went through a very abbreviated version of beer school, and it was transformative. I specifically remember tasting a spontaneously fermented, aged Belgian, and at the time, the idea that I was drinking a beer brewed with stuff that just fell into it blew my mind! I'd never even heard of spontaneous fermentation back then.

DAVE: I was probably the one that taught the class.

MIKE: Really?!

DAVE: Yeah, because that's one of the things I used to do at Oldenberg. I apparently have the gift of gab for beer.

MIKE: Holy shit! Beer Dave gave me my first beer education twenty years before I remember meeting you—before you were even named Beer Dave!

BRET: What strikes me about those early days of beer camp is the ritual that you guys incorporated so much into it.

DAVE: Yeah. Friday night, we would do the unveiling of the brew. We had some of my beer deputies get on either end of the accordion doors. They folded them back, and I'd be standing on this throne welcoming people in. I'd have this inflated beer mug on my head, and while they're coming in, we're playing the theme from *Exodus* like I'm leading them into the Promised Land. You know, we would just do crap like that. On Sunday morning, we would have these little plays. Usually by then, somebody had done something at beer camp that we played on. Even when we bused them out to do the pub tour on Saturday, we'd use school buses. It gave it sort of that summer campness. We kept it all very tongue-in-cheek.

MIKE: One of the ways that a lot of people know you best these days is by doing a weekly segment on Mike McConnell's 700 WLW morning radio show. How did you get started doing radio?

DAVE: Paul Abrams and I used to do the Gary Burbank show. I first did Gary Burbank back in Oldenberg days. Oldenberg was buying some radio time, and if you were one of the people buying radio time, once a month, you had an opportunity to come into the studio and do "Sports or Consequences." One day I got a call, and they said, "We need somebody over to 700 WLW to do Sports or Consequences." I'm like, "Well, I don't know a lot about sports." They told me, "That's all right—they'll do some beer questions." All of a sudden, Gary Burbank said, "Oh, my gosh, they haven't lost a single beer question!" Paul Abrams was working for a company that also advertised on the show, so Paul and I started going to the Burbank show after that. [Gary Burbank was a nationally syndicated radio host on Cincinnati's 700 WLW from 1981 until retiring in 2021.]

Mike McConnell had me on a couple of times to talk beer when he used to do the midday show. He'd be on from noon to three or something like that. We did a couple of hour-long beer shows as well, and then people are like, "Wow, this guy really, really knows beer." It just kind of came from that era, back in probably '89 or something, because I think we tied it in as a way to promote one of the first beer camps, so we've known each other for a long time. McConnell left town to do a show in Chicago for a while, and when he came back from Chicago, he reached out to me and he says, "Hey, what if once a week we did something on beer?" I said, "I'll get you six topics that we can discuss. I'll get you a six-pack of topics every week." Nine o'clock on Friday morning is his five o'clock, so we decided to start doing it as the last ten minutes of his show. It's like I'm sending him off with some marching orders for the weekend—things to go do. And it's become a great little avenue to talk about brewery anniversaries, new beers coming out, new breweries opening and other industry topics. I could probably do it twice a week with no problems anymore. It's been a good way to take all the news of the week and cram it into this little six- or seven-minute segment. I'm amazed at how the segment's grown, that people recognize my voice, or they'll say, "I don't miss a show on Friday." It's just kind of comical, something so simple.

MIKE: I met Mike McConnell for the first time around 2007. We were going to start doing an annual event that was basically a rip-off of the Great Guinness Toast except to Christian Moerlein, on Fountain Square. We got several celebrity judges, and McConnell was one of them. There was a possibility of rain, so we rented a tent for the judges, had them covered and thought that we'd prepared for the worst-case scenario, but this rain was epic!

DAVE: I know which event you're talking about. Oh my God! It was a deluge.

MIKE: Absolutely. Noah and the Arc, eighty-mile-per-hour, horizontal rain. Everybody got soaked. McConnell got soaked. We prepared for rain, but we didn't know a hurricane was coming to Cincinnati. A few years ago, I ran into him at an event I did in Glendale. He came up to me afterwards, was very nice, and he introduced himself. I'd done his show a few times over the years for Bockfest, but it was always phone interviews, and he didn't remember me. He suggested that I do a segment or two on his show. I said, "Absolutely, I'd love to pursue that." Then, because I thought that it would be a fun bonding moment, I reminded him of that rain event. I thought, it's been over ten years, so this is just an amusing recollection that we can laugh about together. Instead, he gave me this stone-cold "fuck you" look, quickly ended the conversation, walked away and didn't respond to the follow-up e-mails that he told me to send. Apparently, it's still too soon for him.

BRET: How long have you been doing the McConnell show?

DAVE: It'll be eight years in October 2023. Never missed a Friday. I've done it from all over the place in my travels, in the hotel room or from the car, pull over and do the segment and move on. It's been good fun, and it forces me to stay up to date and in tune with what's going on with breweries.

BRET: How many breweries have you been to?

DAVE: Almost five thousand in the U.S., and that's over half of all the breweries that are currently open in the U.S. Somebody has to be the guy that, when they throw dirt on top of him, he got to more than anybody else. They always do those segments on ESPN about these four college kids that are going to all the ballparks. Whatever. I'm like, well, when you've been to five thousand breweries, we'll talk.

BRET: Do you have a favorite?

A young, still pie-eyed Beer Dave—back when he was plain old Dave Gausepohl—posing in Oldenberg's Beer Museum. *Courtesy of the Kenton County Public Library, Covington, Kentucky.*

DAVE: Hopefully I haven't been there yet because that would mean that I've crossed the finish line already. Same with beer. I have styles that I like, but there are styles that are still in some guy's head. I hope that the man or the woman who is going to open the best brewery or brew the best beer isn't even born yet. Look at what's happened in ten years. Ten years is not much in our lifetime, but look at what's happened in the beer scene in Cincinnati in that ten years. It's hard to believe, and we're clearly not finished.

BRET: Has there been a worst brewery?

DAVE: Probably the one beer I wouldn't try. I was at a brewery getting ready to sample the guy's beers, and when he went over to test the temperature of the mash, he broke a thermometer—a mercury thermometer—and he says, "Oh, not again." I quickly realized I probably don't need to try this guy's beers. And so that's probably the only brewery where I didn't even try a beer. I was like, "Oh, yeah, I just remembered I have to get going." They didn't last much longer. They were one of the early ones in the Bay Area that kind of came and went.

MIKE: What's the first thing that comes to mind when I ask for a story from your years of beer travel?

DAVE: My favorite brush with greatness was in the Atlanta airport. I'm with our Lexington sales manager at the time for Heidelberg Distributing, where I currently work. He's looking back towards the trams and I'm looking towards the gates, and he says, "Don't look now, but I think the guy that's going to come by is Robert Plant." And it was Robert Plant. I was like, "Well, let me go get us a couple autographs." So, I grab a couple of business cards and I go over, and I said, "Mr. Plant, if I could get a couple autographs, I'll leave you alone." He says, "I have an e-mail, a text and a phone call to make; after that I'm all yours." I go sit off to the side. I'm not taking pictures or anything. I don't want people to realize who it is. Then he just kind of waves me over, and I handed him the business card. I said, "I appreciate your time. Thanks for the autographs." He says, "So, where are you headed?" I said, "I'm headed to London," and he says, "Me as well." I said, "Well, you might be on a different section of the plane." Robert Plant replies, "We'll get there at the same time, not to worry." Then he asks, "So what takes you there?" I said, "I won a sales contest for selling Fuller's beer, and me and the sales manager are going to be hosted by Fuller's, and we're going to go watch the Pittsburgh Steelers and the Minnesota Vikings play on Sunday in Wembley Arena." He was like, "Fuller's. Oh, we used to try and get Fuller's in our room when we would travel in the States, and only in the big cities could we get it because it just wasn't readily available." He asked what else we were going to do while in London. I said that on Saturday night, we have a free night and we're going to go over to Hackney, an area of London that's kind of like Brooklyn, sort of a Bohemian area. I said, "There's a brewery over there that I haven't been to yet. They're making American-style craft beer, and they're making American-style barbecue. I think it'd be fun to see what the British spin is on this stuff." He asks, "Is it Duke's Brew and Que?" I said that it is. He says, "My son Logan is their brewer."

So, I spent forty-five minutes talking beer with Robert Plant at the Atlanta airport and I never asked him a single Led Zeppelin question, but I think I struck a nerve with him. I'm sure he appreciated not having to answer a single Led Zeppelin question, and I think that's why I got the time with him because he was probably like, "This guy is interested in something that I'm interested in." He talked to me about the style of beer that he wanted us to drink. He said, "I'd like you to order the Neck Oil." I asked, "What's Neck Oil?" He said, "Well, it's a black IPA," which were popular at the time, "but it's done in tribute to my father, because when we would be on the road and traveling, my father would always tell me, 'Son, if you want my respect, I need to see you break a little neck oil.' You know, some elbow grease, but the

British term is neck oil, to get the ring around the collar, show that you've busted your hump, so to speak." In tribute to [the brewer's] grandfather, he named his black IPA Neck Oil. I had to drink it. I mean, Robert Plant recommended it. So, there's been some really cool moments like that doing this all these years.

SAM ADAMS AND THE 1990s MASSACRE

Beer Dave Gausepohl's long, deep romance with brewing is a great personal story, but in our conversation with Dave about Oldenberg Brewery, he touched on a broader, national phenomenon: the sudden cessation of craft beer's growth in the 1990s. It turns out that the collapse of the industry in the '90s and early 2000s isn't as complicated as we expected. It has one root cause. We talked to Dave about what the '90s looked like locally. Then we moved to the man who was at ground zero of the catastrophe: Jim Koch, founder of Boston Beer Company, the maker of Sam Adams.

❖ ❖ ❖

DAVE: Oldenberg was ahead of his time. They were killing it. They absolutely were. I think if the family would have been able to hold it all together, Oldenberg would have been the Sierra Nevada of the Midwest. The beer was spot on for what was needed in the market at the time. Then, in the mid-'90s, the media turned because they were like, "Well, these microbreweries aren't advertising with us," and the national brewers were all like, "But we are, so we need you to take care of a problem." There was a famous *Dateline NBC* piece where they talked about, you know, before you drink your next beer, make sure you watch *Dateline NBC*. Basically, they were shilling for their advertisers for the Super Bowl, because NBC had just signed a contract to broadcast the Super Bowl for a number of years. The people that were going to advertise during the Super Bowl were saying, "OK, we need a hit piece that's going to go after craft beer." They're like, "Sam Adams is made in this factory, they're contract brewing, paying somebody else to make their beer. We make all of our beer." It was a David and Goliath kind of a thing.

BRET: Mike talked to Jim about that exact hit piece.

DAVE: Yeah, that was the year that I became the first craft beer buyer ever in the world at Party Source. Now there's craft beer buyers at gas stations. But at that time, in 1995, I was in national publications. Then, all of a sudden, this piece hit. It was like, oh, this is awesome. (That's sarcasm.)

MIKE: You were paying close attention to what was going on across the industry. What were the big patterns that emerged in the '90s.

DAVE: In the '90s, a lot of places went out, and I referred to it as a kind of cleansing. Unfortunately, we lost some good breweries that were under-capitalized and were making good beers, but we also lost a lot of things that needed to just go away, like Beer Across America and some of those mail-order things.

◆ ◆ ◆

JIM KOCH, FOUNDER OF BOSTON BEER COMPANY

Jim Koch and Rhonda Kallman founded Boston Beer Company in 1984. Jim and his flagship beer, Sam Adams Boston Lager, transformed the craft beer industry. Unlike the modern beer barons of craft who preceding him, Jim didn't start brewing on some cobbled-together, glorified homebrew system. He contract brewed, meaning that he rented space from an established brewery. This let him produce a consistent, high-quality beer while also minimizing initial capital investment in the early years. It was a brilliant, innovative way of breaking into the industry, and Boston Beer was wildly successful. But the strategy that helped the company catch its footing and grow became a latent public relations vulnerability, one that helped bring the entire craft brewing industry to a screeching halt for about a decade.

When we started doing *Brew Skies Happy Hour* podcast, Jim Koch was one of the people that we knew we needed to interview. However, we kept striking out in our attempts to make contact. Then, one Saturday, Mike was drinking at Arnold's. A few beers in, he decided to start boring the guy next to him about the podcast, which led to the trials and tribulations of trying to stalk Jim Koch. Cincinnati can be a very small town, and it also happens to be Jim Koch's hometown. As luck would have it, the stranger at the bar is a friend of Jim's, and he offered to introduce us. Weeks passed with no response to follow-up e-mails, until one day we got word that Jim would be in town for a wedding, and he had agreed to come into our studio for an interview. The full interview is available in episodes 18–20 of the *Brew Skies Happy Hour* podcast, but when Beer Dave brought up the infamous *Dateline* segment that produced ripple effects big enough to stunt Oldenberg's growth, we decided to use a small excerpt of our Jim Koch interview here too.

By the early '90s, Boston Beer Company composed 30 percent of the American craft market, but craft was still a tiny percentage of the overall beer market. Nevertheless, the behemoth Anheuser-Busch, under the reigns of August Busch III, made destroying Boston Beer a major priority.

◆ ◆ ◆

MIKE: So, what happened?

JIM: I pissed him off.

MIKE: How? What did you do to August Busch III?

JIM: Well, I know the specific moment. We won the Great American Beer Festival (GABF) for three years in a row. Then there was a year where we didn't enter, and then we won a fourth year, so Charlie Papazian (who founded GABF) said, "Well, you can call it four years running." And I went, "Okay, good." We had a banner with that, and it was in a beer distributor's warehouse. They put the different brand banners up, and some of them had Elvira and things like that. Ours said, "The best beer in America, winner of the Great American Beer Festival." They'd been up there for a few years. So, August III goes on vacation in Hawaii, and he thought of these independent beer distributors like my distributor, and rightly so. He made them very rich.

I had total respect for the man. He was passionate. He cared about quality. He cared about winning. Winning in business—that's an important trait— and doing it in a way that he considered honorable.

MIKE: You've noted that Budweiser is very consistent, very good for what it is.

JIM: He tasted samples every day from different breweries. He had a will of iron. He wiped out a significant portion of the German hop growing industry, the part that made one of the five noble hops. Hersbrucker was a primary hop in Budweiser, and he got, "a head feeling" from samples that had more Hersbrucker in it. He paid off his hop contracts and stopped using it out of quality concerns. So, right or wrong, you have to respect the guy.

He was in Hawaii, but isn't laying on the beach—he's inspecting the warehouse of his wholesaler there to make sure they're meeting his standards, the beer is kept cold, you can eat off the floor, all those things, and he sees this banner and he stops. He looks, he points up at it and he asks the general manager, "Do you think Sam Adams is the best beer in America?" The guy said, "I don't know, I'm just the beer distributor. They give us a point of sale." August wouldn't let up. He says, "Do you think Sam Adams is the best beer in America?" and this goes on. August refuses to move: "I am standing here until you take that blah, blah, blah, banner off the wall of this warehouse," and he stood there while they had to get some big crane and move pallets of beer and take the banner down.

MIKE: The guy's richer than God at this point, and he threw a fit over a banner in a Hawaii distributor's warehouse?

JIM: Actually, he was doing well, but the family had so many kids, and they loved having kids, so the ownership was so fragmented. He had less than 1 percent, I think, but relatively, he had plenty of money.

MIKE: He wasn't in fear of living under a bridge.

JIM: No, he wasn't Bill Gates, but he was doing just fine. That began what Paul Shipman at Red Hook—which had been acquired by Anheuser-Busch—what Paul called, with some glee, the "ethnic cleansing." That was a little frightening because the most powerful man in the entire global business of beer has decided that Jim Koch needs to be ethnically cleansed. He's probably had a trench dug somewhere for me. It was a little bit scary because a guy that I knew had been very, very high up in Anheuser-Busch, and he gave me advice. He said, "You know, Jim, don't park your car in really dark places. Be really careful late at night." I'm like, "You must be paranoid." He said, "No, after I left AB, before I went through security at the airport, I always opened my luggage and made sure nobody had planted drugs." Wow! I thought he must be paranoid, but he was on the executive committee there. It was called ABIS, and he was issuing the hits before he was scared.

MIKE: What was ABIS?

JIM: Anheuser-Busch Investigative Services. It hired like ex-FBI people.

MIKE: Budweiser has its own FBI?

JIM: Yeah. The ex-head of the FBI was on their board. So, then I realized, "Oh, shit, this is real!" I can't believe it to this day, but what I was told is, it wouldn't happen directly, but maybe in a meeting with the Teamsters, August might just drop a, you know, "I wouldn't mind if somebody beat the crap out of Jim Koch." Oh, okay. You drop a hint in front of the right people and shit happens. So, it was an interesting time, but the end of the story is that I'm still here, and he's all gone.

MIKE: Yes, he is all gone.

JIM: He lost his company. He's stomping around at Grant's Farm. I'm told he now has a roller board given to him by the Heineken family. He made fundamental, strategic mistakes by thinking I was the enemy. I remember talking to a very senior AB guy at a brewing conference, trying to talk a little bit of sense into him, not realizing this was a holy war. I said, "I'm not August's enemy. I'm a little American brewer, not a threat. You have enemies, but those enemies are in Dublin and in Brazil, and in places you may not even know about like China, because this business is gonna globalize and you have the opportunity to lead it and think really big, and you're trying to kill little Jim Koch when you've got a big global game getting played out. And I'm not sure that you are winning at that."

MIKE: And you were right—globalization is what kicked his ass.

Jim Koch, Boston Beer Company founder and creator of Sam Adams Boston Lager, drinking beer and answering questions in the *Brew Skies* studio. *Courtesy of Dan Phenicie, 7/79 Video Productions.*

JIM: Yeah, a bunch of very smart, very tough, very strategic Brazilians outsmarted and outmaneuvered him and took his company away. I honestly think that was a big loss for American brewing. As much as he tried to put me out of business, I was very sad when that happened.

MIKE: When you go to St. Louis and talk about beer culture there, it is interesting. For all of Anheuser-Busch's faults, they were still an American company. They still cared a lot about St. Louis, which is not something that you can say about AB-InBev.

JIM: No, that's not their business model. So, yeah, it was a loss for St. Louis, it was a loss for America, but it's business. He got outsmarted. It's a warning for anybody in business. As dominant as they were, there was a bunch of guys from what, at the time, was a third-world country, plotting a good five years in advance. That wasn't a spur-of-the-moment grab. They were totally strategic. If you're gonna be in business, you don't take a day at the beach. There's always somebody who may be smarter and hungrier and tougher and more resourceful out there, and maybe they're a little bit luckier too. Arrogance is a dangerous thing. My grandmother told me several times: humility is a virtue.

MIKE: What did Anheuser-Busch attack you for?

JIM: Well, they went after us on every front. In this ethnic cleansing, we got kicked out of dozens of Anheuser-Busch wholesalers in very short order, just dropped, and had to scramble to find new distributors. They would go after our point of sale.

MIKE: My family used to own an IGA, a small grocery store in Appalachian Ohio. When Walmart moved in, they told the Pepsi distributorships, "You can service those small guys or you can service us, but you can't do both." Was that essentially what they did with the distributors?

JIM: Oh, they didn't even have to be that subtle. August would say, "Show your loyalty. You have 100 percent share of mind from us. We need 100 percent share of mind from you." It was literally a campaign, and they graded wholesalers, A, B, C and D. You can't blame them. They made these guys rich. They owed August that fealty. I don't hold it against them that they showed loyalty to the person who had done so much for them and their families. When the time came, they did the right thing and screwed me. I'm a grown up.

MIKE: I respect your bigness, but some of this sounds like pretty shitty behavior to me.

JIM: I think people are inherently good, and that is my interpretation of their behavior. Some of them are my distributors again, and I'm not gloating. Welcome back. They were good people when I appointed them, and they didn't become bad people because they did what their primary supplier wanted them to do. They would tear our point of sale displays down in markets. They'd move our shelves. It was kind of hand-to-hand combat. Then they went to the federal government and petitioned that you'd have to put the name of your contract producer on the beer label instead of your name. Mine would have had to say, "Made by Pittsburgh Brewing."

MIKE: This was an attack on Boston Beer because you were still contract brewing everything at that stage of your business?

JIM: At that point, yes. That was right before we bought the Cincinnati Brewery here, and I had always put Pittsburgh on the label as the brewing location, which we didn't have to do. Anheuser-Busch didn't put Houston, Texas, or Merrimack, New Hampshire, on their labels. They just put St.

Louis, even though it wasn't made in St. Louis. I always put the brewing location, and our contracts had always given us complete control of the brewing process and the product. So, to me it was misleading to put "Brewed by Pittsburgh Brewing" on a label when they had zero control over the ingredients, the product, the process, et cetera. BATF [Bureau of Alcohol Tobacco and Firearms] looked at their petition and said, "That makes no sense." They didn't even review it, but it's actually still an active petition. They never withdrew it, and if you look at all these craft brewers that Anheuser-Busch bought, not a single one says "Brewed by Anheuser-Busch"—not one. If I were a little more of a jerk than I actually am, I'd be supporting Anheuser-Busch's petition. "Yeah, that's a great idea! Let's do that! Why don't you require that of people?"

Then they started a national advertising attack campaign claiming that I was tricking consumers. It was around Halloween, and the ghost of Sam Adams came to my door [in a commercial]. They had a fake Jim Koch voice, and Sam Adams was mad that I was deceiving people, blah, blah, blah.

MIKE: Because rather than having a big brewery somewhere, you were still doing contract brewing?

JIM: That's right.

MIKE: Even though you were still entirely using your own brewers, making your own beer with your own recipes, and Boston Beer employees were managing and overseeing every step of the production process?

JIM: Yes, exactly. I had a lawyer in Minnesota call me, and he said, "I just heard that ad. That is an illegal ad. It is false and misleading, and you should sue them."

MIKE: Sometimes lawyers help.

JIM: Yeah. I called my lawyer who incorporated me, but he's not an advertising lawyer or anything, and I said, "I think this ad is misleading." He said, "Jim, it doesn't matter." I said, "What do you mean it doesn't matter? Can I sue Anheuser-Busch?" My lawyer, Fred, said, "Jim, do you play polo?" "What do you mean, Fred? Do I play polo? Of course I don't play polo." Then he said, "Well, if you don't play polo, you can't afford to sue Anheuser-Busch." So, I went back to the first lawyer, and he said, "You don't have to sue them. The Better Business Bureau has an arm called the National Advertising Bureau that is set up to adjudicate these disputes outside of the full legal process, and it's very well respected. If they find against Anheuser-Busch, the FTC is very likely to write them and tell them to stop running this ad, and if they don't, the FTC will sue them for you." So, I took it through the adjudication mechanism of the Better Business Bureau—and we won. They had to retract it and change it, but by that time all the damage was done.

MIKE: The retraction is never as big as the allegation.

JIM: Yeah, we got tiny articles. Then there was a *Dateline NBC* story that turned out to be a real hit piece. It went right after craft brewing, and they teased it during the World Series: "Before you buy another pricey microbrew, there's something you should know. Watch *Dateline NBC* on Tuesday." It was a hit piece. I had a friend who had worked at General Electric, and at that time General Electric owned NBC. I asked him to plead my case to a very senior person at GE. The answer we got was, "Look, we can't really make money on the Olympics without Anheuser-Busch....You're probably not gonna like the way the piece comes out, but we're not changing it."

MIKE: Welcome to modern American journalism.

JIM: Chris Hansen—who later got thrown off the air for something unsavory, I don't remember what—did his job really well. The way they edited it and even lit me. I had this dark shadow lighting on my face. I was like, "Oh, this is not gonna come out well." It came out as: "Who's killing you with beer?" Yeah, that's right. "What poisons are gonna be in that pricey craft beer?" It did exactly what they intended. It was incredibly effective. The growth rate of craft beer, the entire industry, went from 25 percent to zero within six weeks. I've never seen anything like that in a consumer product other than carcinogenic tainting. Craft beer didn't grow again from October of '96 until about 2004.

MIKE: Doing the *Brew Skies Happy Hour* podcast, we've had the conversation a lot about what the hell happened in the '90s, why the industry seemed to fall off a cliff. It seems that a lot of what caused so much stagnation and a downturn that killed off hundreds of breweries is largely traceable to a very effective campaign by Anheuser-Bush to quash craft beer. It's crazy

Mike pretending to be BFFs with Jim Koch, who definitely doesn't even remember who he is. *Courtesy of Adam Rabinowitz.*

that one brewery was powerful enough to have such a detrimental effect on the entire industry.

JIM: Yeah, to almost stop a cultural movement, because, yes, craft beer is a business, but at its foundation, it's a cultural movement. It's part of an artisan culture. They couldn't kill it. It was too strong for them to kill it, but they were able to stop the growth for eight long years.

MIKE: Yeah, that's a lot of damage.

JIM: Yeah, but we're still here, and we're sitting here drinking great beer. It's okay—it all has a happy ending.

❖ ❖ ❖

Well, not for everybody. A few of Jim Koch's references merit some follow-up. August Busch III was muscled out of control of Anheuser-Busch by his son, August Busch IV, who was made president of the company in 2006. Through a combination of hubris, incompetence and substance abuse, IV lost the family company in a hostile takeover by InBev in 2008.

After playing such a pivotal role in crippling the nascent craft beer industry with his *Dateline* hatchet-piece interview of Jim Koch on October 13, 1996, Chris Hansen hit the peak of his career hosting *To*

Catch a Predator. Busting would-be sexual predators on live TV proved incredibly popular, but not everybody was a fan. Hansen was accused of being so enthusiastic about producing a show that his affiliates entrapped people in ways that made successfully prosecuting would-be predators impossible, arguably gave pedophiles a course on how to avoid getting caught and possibly ruined innocent lives, including an assistant prosecutor in Texas who committed suicide after being targeted by the show. Controversy forced the show off the air in 2008. Hansen persisted in resurrecting his career as a sleazy, gotcha TV "journalist" but never caught another foothold, and he faced a major additional setback when he was arrested for passing a bad check in 2019.

DAN LISTERMANN

Amateurs Go Pro—Sort Of

Dan Listermann is an engineer who turned a homebrewing hobby into a manufacturing and retail career. Then, he turned that into one of Cincinnati's earliest, modern craft breweries. Along the way, he contributed heavily to the local popularity of homebrewing and, both intentionally and otherwise, helped train some of the region's best commercial brewers.

◆ ◆ ◆

MIKE: When did you start brewing?

DAN: Let's start with the first disaster. I was at Miami University in 1973, and I walked into a drugstore in uptown and there was this bag with a label on it, "Beer Kit." It was illegal to make beer at that time, but it was like a pound of crushed malt, an ounce of hops and instructions. Yeah, sure, why not? So, I got that, and I boiled it up with five pounds of cane sugar, somehow separated the solids from everything else and put that into a new garbage can. I didn't have proper yeast, so I ended up using Fleischmann's. Well, if you like hefeweizen, that's what it tasted like, only stranger.

I bought a hydrometer that had a big red "B" on it, a line. That was when you were supposed to bottle it, at a certain point in time when it went down, so I did that. Most of the bottle caps ended up flying all over the place. Some of the bottles broke. It was pretty bad. There was a guy in the frat who was a six-foot albino, musical genius, and he was known to be able to ingest anything. He downed a whole quart of it, and that was quite remarkable. The rest ended up in the fire extinguishers. I did it a few more times, but it got worse. The garbage can got contaminated. I didn't know. So, I quit it. Then, about 1988, my old roommate Brian Johnson, who was the best man at our wedding, called me and said, "Hey, let's make some beer."

My brother and I went up to his place in Camden, and we made some beer. We bottled it, and it was just delicious, and that was the beginning of the end of my engineering career. I started brewing beer.

BRET: I've heard that you were one of the original members of the Bloatarian Brewing League, a local homebrew club that was one of the first in the U.S. Is that accurate?

DAN: I found the Bloatarians, jeez, I wanna say '88 or '89? When were the Bloatarians founded? I believe it was '87—pretty early for a homebrew club. We would meet at the Drawbridge Inn [adjacent to Oldenberg Brewery]. We didn't have any scheduled meetings. There were no officers. About 10:00 on a Thursday night, you'd get a call that we're having a meeting tomorrow at a certain room inside the building. They gave us the rooms for free. It was kinda nice, not being scheduled. We outgrew that eventually.

MIKE: It's nice that Oldenberg was giving you free space. Beer Dave has told us that the brewery used to use the Bloatarians at their events, and it seems like a very symbiotic relationship, everybody kind of learning from each other.

DAN: Oldenberg was doing those beer tastings, which were really cool. In those days, the thought of being able to taste three hundred beers at one time was astounding! I used to go brew beer with Dave Gausepohl on Saturday mornings, otherwise known as Beer Dave. It wasn't like you got to watch Dave brew beer. He put you to work, you know. "Dump this! Turn that!" It was a lot of fun. Can I tell you a quick story about Dave?

MIKE: Sure. We love Dave's stories.

DAN: I was putting a connection to my septic tank in at the camp. I was digging this hole, and I popped up with this Hudy Delight can. The custom in the neighborhood is they drink beer constantly, and then they throw the cans in holes. I didn't know how old my camp was, so I called Dave up, and I described the can over the phone. Dave says, "That's '79 to '81"—just from talking to him over the phone. Later, I brought the can to him, and he says, "Oh, that's '79. I can tell by the curved shoulder and the continental can logo." So, I dated the construction of my camp by can-o-chronology.

BRET: How did you make the leap from homebrewing to abandoning your engineering career?

DAN: I was a manufacturing engineer, and I didn't like the bottle fillers that were offered commercially. They had a foot valve, and you would fill the bottle up, and when you took your foot off, they would suck in two inches of air. They would displace the volume with two inches of air, and I thought that was a problem. I sat in the bar one night, and I designed a better one, just in my head. The next day, I went out to a hobby shop, and I bought the bits of brass tubing and stuff, and I went into the basement and built one.

Dan Listermann building things and wreaking havoc at his riverfront camp. Yes, that does, in fact, appear to be a large gas line being piped into that blazing fire pit. *Courtesy of Roxanne Westendorf.*

I thought, "Oh, that's nice." So, I built a bunch of them, and I gave some out at a Bloatarian meeting. I thought, I could do a lot of these, you know? I talked to the wife about it—my wife has been so incredibly supportive all these years—and she thought it was fun. [Sue Listermann is Dan's wife and business partner.] I always wanted to be in business for myself. So, I told her, "We need to spend this amount of money to buy this stuff"—$1,300, I think. And she said, "Sure." I made stuff in my basement for about six or eight months. Then we started renting a small space in Norwood because I was doing things with buckets and stuff at that point, expanding into lauter tuns and selling them all over the country, all over spots around the world. We went into production there, and in a little while, we ended up with, 1,100 square feet on the third floor.

At that time, the only homebrew supply stores were run by a very disagreeable person up in Kenwood who didn't care about beer at all and a guy over in South Fairmont who worked out of his basement. You called him up, you'd go over there, knock on the door, you'd walk by mom and the dog, you'd go down in the basement and he really didn't have a whole lot, especially for advanced brewers. I thought, "Well, here's an opportunity to make a homebrew shop." Then I needed a place where I could do both the homebrew shop and the manufacturing. That's when we started the homebrew shop up in '95, and that's the location of what became the original brewery.

MIKE: That's how you went from being an engineer to a manufacturer and retailer. How did you become a professional brewer?

DAN: A woman from Middletown called me one day and says she's got this brewing equipment for sale. Her husband had bought it for a bar in Port Clinton, Ohio. They were using it as a token brewery to get an alcohol license, but it didn't work out very well. She gave me a number, $5,000, something like that. It wasn't a whole lot. So, we brought it down, set it up, and we were having a good time with it. That was 2007, something like that? Yeah.

The only time the wife ever balked is when we first got the brewery going. I was the brewer, and it wasn't that good. At that time, the license was $4,000. It was coming up, and she says, "No, no, no, I'm not gonna spend that. This has gotta stop." It was the first time she ever said no to me like that. I said, "Sweetheart, I got $14,000 worth of beer in the back that I can't sell without that license." She did the higher math in her head.

Kevin Moerland, Jason Brewer and Dan Listermann hanging out at Blank Slate. *Courtesy of Scott LaFollette.*

After that, we hired Kevin Moreland, who was really pivotal in getting the quality right.

MIKE: When you started brewing in 2007, you couldn't sell on premises even with a $4,000 license, right?

DAN: No, and we were self-distributing, and all hand bottling.

MIKE: What were keg and bottle sales like in those first years?

DAN: Well, if you wanted to sell the beer, you went out and knocked on doors.

MIKE: How was it received?

DAN: Not well. That's work. You gotta admire people who do that. It's hard putting yourself out there and then getting told to your face, "I don't like it."

That's not my bag, I'm an engineer. I don't do that. Moreland was another matter, though. He has that. So, we did very, very well together.

BRET: I've heard Kevin get credited for developing Nutcase and Chacao, two of your best-known beers.

DAN: Oh yeah. Chacao was like, "Okay, guys, just get it out of your system. I don't wanna hear about it anymore, okay?" And that took off, then Nutcase. I first found out about Nutcase when I walked into the tasting room and saw it on tap, but I was happy. I was happy so long as there's something that normal people could drink,

BRET: Nutcase is a peanut butter porter, and Chacao is a pastry stout. A lot of people have those now, but when you guys started brewing those beers, those styles weren't a thing yet. Whether you like those styles or not, those beers are very good examples of them. You were far ahead of the curve. You also started doing big release parties with Chacao and some of the beers in the Moreland era.

DAN: Yeah, we started doing those parties. That would have been like 2012. Those were a lot of fun, but we got a reputation for doing them in the rain. One time we were ankle deep in the parking lot. Then we found out that was illegal, so we had to have a physical barrier between the brewery license and the festival permit area. We had to switch up to the hill, which was better because it drained, but the rain still came.

BRET: Again, ahead of the curve though. When we first opened in 2015, when I first moved here to Cincinnati, your quarterly festivals were some of the first that I went to.

DAN: They were great. We did German bands. There was a guy called Otto Bond, and he's crazy. He's a one-man-band deal. Somebody has to shoot him with a tranquilizer gun at the end of the event. But every time we did it, they made less and less money. We started to realize that everybody and his damn brother has a festival now, and people got festivaled out.

MIKE: What happened in 2012, when the taproom law changed? Did you immediately take advantage of it?

DAN: We got a cooler, put it in the hallway going back to the homebrew shop, and that was the bar. That was a big investment from our perspective. Yeah, that was really a revolution. It changed the nature of my business a whole lot when it happened. We put the bar in the tasting room where it is now and knocked the walls out where the offices were. Can I tell you about the bar?

MIKE: Absolutely. It's a beautiful bar.

DAN: My great-great-grandfather Martin Listermann had a bar on Spring Grove Avenue at the Mill Creek by St. Bernard; 1875 is when he started it. His grandson sold it in 1968, and they destroyed it for a parking lot. It was a big deal, Listermann Café, and a relative who was an artist did a painting of it in 1954 as it was supposed to appear in 1889. Another relative still has a painting. It's like four feet by eight feet—it's huge. He invited us over to look at that, and I said "Ooh, this is nice." So, when we built the bar, I basically used that design to build it, and I'm really quite proud of that. It's a re-creation of the family bar.

BRET: I'm sure that you've heard it before, but local brewers talk about Listermann University, because so many people came through your homebrew store before opening breweries, and so many professional brewers worked at Listermann in early stages of their careers, then went to work at other breweries or opened their own thing.

DAN: "Listerman University"? I hadn't heard that one, I have to tell the wife that. She'll be tickled.

BRET: Yeah, our first employee, Josh Elliott, was brewing for you.

DAN: Right! Tell him that my cat's still alive. He'll be pleased to hear that. Five or six years ago, I was talking to him about my cat, and he said, "He's still alive?" Yeah, little Joey. He came down with an autoimmune thing in his inner ear that is causing infections in his teeth. We medicated him for years and years. I've had him nine years now, and eventually the medication just became less and less effective. My vet said, "If we pull all of his teeth out, there's an 80 percent chance he can get over this." I said, "Good!" and we did.

Listermann Brewing Supplies and Listermann Brewing Company, Norwood, Ohio. *Courtesy of Michael D. Morgan.*

BRET: So, you have a toothless cat?

DAN: I have a toothless cat, yes. I find dead mice that look like they've been run over by something, but they've just been gummed, heavily gummed.

MIKE: I've always loved your brewery, and you guys have produced some really creative beers, but I'm not going to pretend to get all of them. First there was a Gatorade beer. It tasted exactly like Gatorade, and I thought, that's fun. Then the next time I went in, there were either three or four different Gatorade beers, and I thought, hmm, that seems a bit excessive.

DAN: My brewers started to ignore the more conventional beers, and that got to be a problem. Everything had to be weird. I appreciate weird, but I want to make sure that when somebody walks into my door, that they have something they can feel comfortable drinking. There are always weird things on our beer menu, and people will have one, but they won't come back and they won't say nice things about you. If you make your name pushing these things, there's only one direction to go—crazy or crazy—you have to keep getting crazier. Where's the sustainability in that?

BRET: What was the first really great beer you remember having, something that inspired you?

DAN: Christian Moerlein. It was a Vienna style, I believe. [This is a reference to the craft beer released by the Hudepohl Brewing Company in 1981.] That was an epiphany. It was the first time beer ever tasted really delicious to me. I quit buying it because I would drink all of it. If I bought a six-pack, it was gone, and I felt like shit the next day. It was really, really good. Sometimes the worst part about beer is the fact that it has alcohol in it because I just want to drink buckets of good beer. Then you wake up, you feel like shit. I literally stopped buying it because I had to go to work.

MIKE: When you built your first bottle filler, did you have any idea of the ride that lay ahead?

DAN: People ask me, "Dan, how did you plan all this?" Plan? "Well, I'm an engineer," I say, "and there are drawings from every step of the way." It just all happened. Right now, my camp is my life.

◆ ◆ ◆

In February 2023, Dan and Sue Listermann retired. They sold Listermann Brewing Company to husband-and-wife team Steve and Terrie Ipson. The Listermanns retained ownership of the real estate, and Dan has been providing consulting services. Dan spends most of his time at his "camp," a cabin on the White Water River. He's enjoying retirement but never stops working on projects, solving problems—even when he has to create the problem first. When we recorded this interview in the spring of 2023, he was dedicating most of his brain power to designing and building a floating hot tub, sunken to be flush to the top of his boat dock. Plans involve repurposing a three-hundred-gallon watering trough and a 1913 hot water heater. (Dan: "Ah, Jesus! I have big parties out there, and I thought, this place needs a hot tub.")

Dan also explained that he has moderated his lifestyle and barely drinks anymore, almost never drinking more than two beers in a night. That's great, and we're very supportive of those decisions, but he said this as we were handing him his third beer. After the interview concluded, Dan wanted to stop in and say hi to Mike Kemp, the proprietor and brewer at Humble Monk Brewing Company, across the street from the *Brew Skies* studio and Urban Artifact. We showed him the way and then went to check on him about an hour later, around 5:00 p.m. He was beginning to insist on speaking partly in German to people who don't speak a word of German, which is something that he does when he starts catching a nice buzz. We're told that he stayed until after 10:00 p.m. and that by the end of the night, he was entirely refusing to speak English. Sorry, Dan. Sometimes we break people.

SCOTT LaFOLLETTE

The Blank Slate Experiment

Starting work on a small production brewery, built largely with his own hands, Scott LaFollette opened Blank Slate Brewing Company in 2012 in a strip of industrial buildings near Lunken Airport. Blank Slate was a revolution in beer styles and flavor. LaFollette is still regarded as one of the most talented brewers in the Cincinnati regional scene, and beer geeks can get doe-eyed and wistful recollecting their favorites among his creations. Nevertheless, although Blank Slate poured arguably the best liquid in the business at the time, and the brewery opened at the moment that the local craft beer market was poised to explode, Blank Slate struggled and closed its doors in 2017.

Scott was gracious enough to come into the studio, drink a few foamy beverages and regale us with the good times and the bad, what went right and why things ended wrong. Before we started recording, we were having a random conversation about visiting a local taproom, which lapsed into complaining about kids—other people's kids. Why brewery taprooms seem to be such popular places to bring children is, however, a question that comes up a lot when discussing the space designs and retail aspects of the business. The rant started to get relevant, and we started to record, so let's start there, by waxing philosophical about why children in breweries is so divisive.

❖ ❖ ❖

SCOTT: That place has turned into daycare with a liquor license. From a business standpoint, if it works, great. Infants tend not to drink that much, but their parents wouldn't go anywhere otherwise.

MIKE: The kids in taprooms issue comes up with us a lot. You opened one of the earlier taprooms in the city, and you've seen the growth and evolution of what taprooms have become, so I'd love to get your perspective on how and why it became acceptable to take your toddler to a taproom and behave in a way that wouldn't be acceptable in any other bar.

SCOTT: I think the people who bring their kids in and let them run loose were always there, even in the beginning. There just wasn't nearly as many of them. When we started out, breweries were just some random warehouse. They didn't look like anything else, so why should the rules be the same as anywhere else? There just wasn't as many, but even in the early days you'd still have the occasional people bring their kids and it'd be like, "Hey, go get your kid! What the hell are you doing?" They'd say, "No, he's just playing with the brewing equipment." Oh, yeah. In the early days, most people didn't have very good separations between taproom space and the production space. All the time, you were like, "Get off that." "You can't go back there." "You can't climb that. You can't climb that!" They were always there, but it's gotten worse.

MIKE: It's gotten worse because it's become more accepted?

SCOTT: Right. It's become more accepted because there's so many taprooms. When there were only a few taprooms, everyone was super hardcore about what they wanted their taproom to be. This is what I want the aesthetic to be, the vibe I'm trying to create—what I want to be. It was always the vision of the owner, whether that was right, wrong or for the greater good. You could be as weird and narrow and specialized as you wanted to because no one else was doing it. The next thing you know, you've got ten taprooms in random warehouses, and you're getting the same aesthetic and environment. It's like, "Why am I going to drive past four others to get to yours?" As that's happened, breweries were thinking, "I've got to have some reason for people to come to my place and drive past those other four places." Then you start getting people who are doing more specialty things. The biggest thing in the beginning was food. When the first couple of guys added food, that became why you'd drive past the other four guys to go to that place, because they had

Scott drinking with an infant at an outdoor event, presumably to keep the kid out of the taproom. Alternatively, it's a parent-child bonding moment. *Courtesy of Scott LaFollette.*

food. Then almost all the taprooms were offering food, and you had to start asking yourself, what demographic are we missing? How do you grow this? We have to expand, but what we're about? Instead of being uber focused on doing one kind of thing—which still exists—we've got to appeal to more people. What do we do? We need to appeal to families because that's kind of the big missing demographic. So, taprooms started becoming more and more family friendly, which is how they would build their spaces out, how they were structured, and you know, we better get air conditioning, those kinds of things. We better have food and blah, blah, blah, blah. That allowed more families to start coming in, and they still were not a normal standard restaurant or normal standard bar. The kids started running loose, but hey, they're bringing their parents and they're all drinking and they're buying lots of stuff. So yeah, this sucks, but we can't fuck with it because if all these parents decide not to come here with their kids anymore, we're going to lose a whole bunch of revenue.

BRET: What you're saying, in part, is that competition didn't necessarily breed specialization. It's the other way around. It turned breweries into Applebee's.

SCOTT: I think in some ways it has. If you think about the early days, your weirdness could shine through. Also, why would I want to just do the same thing that an Applebee's can do way better than I can? Why do I want to compete with that? Just like I don't want to be Budweiser. I wanted to be something different, and I think that's what a lot of us were all about in the beginning. We wanted to do something different, not the status quo, whether it's in beer or in the hospitality end of things, and that's what we did. Then you started to basically see the inverse effect. I don't really know who was the first to go more mainstream, but a couple of people didn't have anything super interesting to add, so they went more generic and mainstream. Those breweries very quickly got a lot more consumers to come to them than the ones that started out specialized and stayed specialized. When I started, you got to be different, you got to be unique, got to have something cool. Now, if someone said, "I'm going to start a taproom today, what should I do?" I would honestly say, "Make it look as much like an Applebee's as you can." I'm not saying philosophically, but if you just want to talk dollars and cents, make your beers as approachable to as many people as you can.

MIKE: Yeah, the more breweries we get, the more homogeneous the beer seems to get, which seems counterintuitive.

SCOTT: Yeah, it really does. I don't know if it's necessarily that way everywhere. It definitely didn't used to be that way. I don't know if it's because when we started in Cincinnati, we could look towards California, Colorado, Portland, and we looked at what was there and said, "What's the coolest thing there? That's what I want to do here." Which means that we skipped that evolution of things, starting out kind of small and homogeneous and then diverging out. In Cincinnati, we started with the extremes, and we've worked our way to the middle. At the start, we were like, "I'm not making fizzy yellow beer!" Now, that's what everybody is doing. Everybody wants lagers. How can I make fizzy yellow beer? Fretboard just came out with a beer—no disrespect to them—that they literally put in the press release for, "We're coming after Budweiser with this beer." Who would have said that ten years ago? Ten years ago, it would have made you a pariah.

BRET: Why would you want to do that? It's also a death spiral because you're not going to out-Budweiser Budweiser.

SCOTT: I agree, but we're somehow weirdly working our way back to being more homogeneous so that we can attract more people. We've maxed out the growth that we're going to get from people who are interested in cool, unique experiences because that demographic doesn't grow at the rate that the "normal world" grows.

BRET: How do you feel about sugar-forward beers, and are you proud to have made the first pastry stout?

SCOTT: Fuck you.

BRET: Perfect answer. I'm referring to Opera Cream Stout, which became one of your most popular early beers. It was named after a pastry, but I'm pulling your chain a little because it was a traditional sweet stout with a lot of coffee flavor. Not sickly sweet like modern pastry stouts, but it is the first time that I can recall anyone around here making a beer that tasted like a dessert.

SCOTT: I bear no blame and take no credit for starting the pastry stout. Absolutely not. I don't generally care for the super sickeningly sweet beers. It's a personal preference. Some people do—fine, drink them, have fun with your diabetes, whatever, that's your choice. Obviously, none of those crazes started in this town, but if you look at just the overall evolution of things again, once everybody is making the same kinds of beer, somebody has got to try something different. Those beers grew out of being the total opposite of blast-you-in-the-face, melt-your-tongue-off-IBU IPAs, which is kind of where we got. We had the IBU race, as everyone called it. When you push something to one end, the total polar opposite starts to grow somewhere. It's the yin and the yang, the greater balance or something. I don't know.

BRET: I think that the genericism of the taproom experience led the way to a genericism of flavor profiles, which leads to sugar. If you look at the wine industry, the main driver of wine sales are sweet, sugary wine.

SCOTT: Well, I don't think it was intentional in the beginning, but when people started making those sweeter beers, the pastry styles, and it started appealing to people that weren't into beer, breweries were like, "Oh, this is bringing in new people that never used to come here because they don't like beer, but they'll drink something that tastes like dessert." That's cool because you've saturated out the niche of people that think like you, that want to drink beer like you make it. They're already here, and that group is not growing fast enough for you to be able to grow. You have to bring in more people, and it's either convert them to your will or give them something that they already want. If at the end of the day, you're trying to make money and that helps you make money, great.

I wish we could have figured out another category to call those things so that they didn't have to be called beer. Everything can exist, but if I'm trying to make a really nice, classic, Czech pilsner or something, and you come around with this syrupy, godawful mess of adjuncts, and they're both called beer? I don't know if I agree with that. I'm not saying you can't make that, but can we call it something else?

BRET: I agree with you. I support that a 1,000 percent, and I will be the first to say that what I make at Urban Artifact is not beer. It's more beer than some of those pastry stouts are, but some of what we make can be 30 percent to 40 percent fruit. It's not beer to me. It's high adjunct. I'm the first to admit it, and I agree, beer should be protected more.

Beer as a beverage was one of the original foodstuffs with laws defining what it can and cannot be. The *Reinheitsgebot* is often touted as the first modern food safety law. Beer today falls under much looser guidelines, largely driven by corporate lobbying to expand the definition of beer. Beer in America today simply must be made from grain or a grain substitute, such as sugar. By extension, all hard seltzers are legally beer. This is not what we in the industry philosophically or romantically think of as the definition of beer.

BRET: What's the first great beer you've ever had?

SCOTT: Ever? The first beer that I drank that I was like, "Oh, wow, this is what beer can be?" It's kind of a lame story because it's not that exciting of a beer. I was going to college in Cleveland, and weekends were about what we could get the most of. We were drinking Iron City because it was the cheapest thing you could get in Cleveland, oddly enough. Me and my roommate were celebrating. We just passed exams. We went to some bar that we knew we could get into underage, and we're like, "Let's get a fancy beer." The fanciest beer they had on top was Great Lakes Dortmunder. That kind of sent me down the path, even though it's not a huge stretch of a beer, but that started me down the path.

MIKE: That's one of those beers that I tell students is a gateway drug.

SCOTT: Yeah, absolutely. That led to a little beer store down the street that had a decent selection of imports but very little craft. I was a budget drinker. Now, if I'm not going to drink cases of Iron City, I wanted the best bang for my buck. The highest ABV beer they had was Old Peculiar. It was like 7 percent or something. I drank that entire six-pack, and it was great. I was like, "Oh my God, I only had to drink six beers and I'm just as drunk as everybody else here who is a twelve-pack deep." That became my go to beer. We'd go to a college party, and everybody would show up with a twelve-pack of this or a case of this. I'd show up with a six-pack of Old Peculiar. People would laugh and say, "That's all you're going to drink?" I'm like, "Dude, I'm going to drink these six beers, I'm going to be twice as drunk as you and I'm going to pee half as much"—and it tasted great. So those were like my first two.

BRET: You don't need to name the brewery, but on the flip side, what's the worst beer experience you've ever had?

SCOTT: I won't say who it is. I will say they're within a twenty-mile radius of here.

BRET: Don't tell me it's going to be an Urban Artifact beer.

SCOTT: Well, it was kind of sour, but not on purpose. They'd been open for a while, so it wasn't like their first batches. To this day, I can remember this beer. I don't remember what it was supposed to be, but I can remember what it was: the single most off-flavored beer I'd had in my life. From a beer nerd science standpoint, I almost drank the entire thing because I was trying to figure out how you could simultaneously have so many different off-flavors in one beer at the same time. It was diacetyl, it was acetaldehyde, it was oxidized. It had some weird chlorophenol character going on, and it was infected. I just sat there and marveled. I thought, if I tried a hundred times, I couldn't re-create this. If I did everything wrong that I know to do wrong, because some of them were like competing off-flavors, how could it simultaneously be too young and too old? I drank most of it. I had to. It hurt to do it. I had to figure it out because there was something to learn. I remember that beer distinctly to this day.

BRET: What's the dumbest thing you've heard someone say about craft beer?

SCOTT: Oh, good God! Just go to Untapped and start scrolling. I might have to circle back to that one.

BRET: I love scrolling Untapped and seeing people check in on some of our beers with wildly inaccurate things. Not bad opinions, but bad information. In the taproom, I used to try to correct people. I'd hear somebody talking to their buddy and they'd say something wildly incorrect, and I'd insert myself into the conversation. Sometimes people would say, "Cool, thanks for the information," but I quickly realized that most people don't care. They're usually mad that you corrected them in front of their friends. As I've gotten older, I'm not as dumb, I kind of hate it about myself as a beer nerd, but most of the time now, when I hear somebody say something wrong, I just walk the other way.

SCOTT: Anymore, it's just not worth it. Again, it's the evolution of things. In the beginning, we were all very defensive because we were trying to protect the craft. The craft is fucked now.

BRET: Do you think that craft beer is one big family as it claims to be?

SCOTT: Well, maybe it's a divorced family. It's definitely not as much of a family as it was. If you go back to 2014 or 2015, not only did I know all of the guys who started all the breweries in this town, I knew everybody who worked in those breweries. And I knew most of the people who tended bar in this town. Everybody knew everybody. As things have grown and expanded, that's unsustainable. In those days, when somebody was looking to start up, they went around to all the other breweries and got to know people, made friends with the owners, and they were like, "Hey, you got any advice?" That was a big thing, and it was great. I loved it. I was like, "Man, if there's anything I can teach you, ever do to help you out," blah, blah, blah, and I would. Then it went to every other freaking day, some guy is walking in saying, "I'm thinking about starting a brewery," and they'd want to pick your brain. I had to start asking, "Where are you on the process?" If somebody said, "We've been working on a business plan for two years," I'd stop everything I was doing, sit down and talk to them for as long as I possibly could to help. Then you started getting guys coming in with, "Last week, me and a couple of friends were at such-and-such and we said, 'Man, we should start a brewery.' You got any advice?" Yeah, when you've got some specific questions, come back and ask me. I was not as willing to commit as much time unless it was somebody that was serious and had already put a lot of work into it. Then, it just stopped one day. Nobody was coming in and introducing themselves, whether it was the guy who decided last week or it was a guy who was two years into his business plan. Suddenly it became, "Oh, I went and visited ten different taprooms. So, I got this, Dad. Let's go cash out your 401k and start a brewery." They started doing it without going around and talking to anybody, becoming part of that brewing family, so to speak. Some of that is because places started getting bigger, and it became a little harder to come in and get that advice. But also, people were coming from completely outside, and they didn't know anybody. Because of that, yeah, everything's definitely become less of a family because there's just so many people involved now.

MIKE: With a great deal of admiration, Bret and I have referred to you as the Jack McAuliffe of Cincinnati. [Jack McAuliffe started New Albion Brewery, America's first, built-from-scratch craft brewery in Sonoma, California, in 1976. Jack played a critical role in inventing the modern craft beer movement, but he went out of business in 1981, largely because he was ahead of his time. We interview Jack's daughter, Rene Deluca, in episode 2 of *Brew Skies Happy Hour* podcast.]

SCOTT: Oh, man. That might be more Dan Listermann, but I appreciate the comparison. Thank you.

MIKE: Dan may be more accurate in the pure Wild West, building-a-brewery-from-scratch sense, but the comparison comes from McAuliffe's larger story.

Scott LaFollette on his first brew day at Blank Slate. *Courtesy of Scott LaFollette.*

Jack saw the future. He understood what to do, but we often reference the adage "The pioneers get the arrows and the settlers get the land." We also talk a lot about how being smarter than your consumer doesn't pay.

SCOTT: Yes, I would argue I was trying to be too smart, too cute for the market at the time.

MIKE: Which is admirable, but there is a point where being too good at what you're doing screws you up. Being too far ahead of the consumer is problematic.

SCOTT: Yeah, if you want to be successful in business, you've got to give people what they want. You have to balance that with what you want to be, and one of my biggest faults was being too far into the camp of being what I wanted to be and what I wanted to brew. Everything in those days was IPA, IPA, IPA, so I didn't want to do an IPA. If you want a good IPA, I'll send you down the street. There's a hundred of them. I'll send you to the store. There's a hundred good IPAs on the shelf. Why do I want to bother making another IPA? I want to do things that are not already out there, but it doesn't work that way.

MIKE: No, it doesn't, and that's a sad thing. You were making some really brilliant beers, inventive and delicious. Towards the end, when forced, you also did a fantastic IPA.

SCOTT: Yeah, towards the end. When forced. Well, we had done IPAs, but it was not going to be a plain old IPA. I was going to do variations of the IPA: a red IPA, white IPA, black IPA. That was the early days. Then towards the end, I was like, "All right, we're going straight up fucking IPA." And as soon as we did that beer, guess what became the best-selling beer in our taproom? Yeah, IPA. It wasn't until after the fact that I wondered, why was I so stubborn? Why didn't I just make an IPA like everybody else? The biggest guys at the time all had a flagship IPA. I was trying to be too cute. I thought, if I'm the next guy with another flagship IPA, am I gonna be the guy that tips the scale and oversaturates the IPA market? Or do I do different things? As it turns out in the end, I should have just continued to saturate the IPA market. It would have been more profitable, and I've learned now that you can still do the cool thing—I'm not saying I'm ever doing it again!—but if I was doing it over again, I'd understand that there's a set of beers you've got to make, whether you like them or not. You've got to have a decent IPA—you arguably have to have two IPAs, a hazy and a non-hazy now. You've got to have a not just a bullshit blonde ale, ideally, it's a well-done lager, some kind of basic stout at the right time of year. There are things that you've got to have, but it doesn't mean you can't have twelve taps and eight of them are the things you've got to have and the other four are whatever wild ass shit you want to do. You've just got to understand that for every one of that weird stuff, you're going to sell ten beers of the other stuff. If the weirder stuff is where you want to be known, you've just got to understand that that's probably not what's going to keep you alive. You're not going to be wildly successful doing crazy, esoteric beers. There are exceptions, and there are people that have done that. There are always exceptions to the rule, but the rule is the rule for a reason.

BRET: Our distributor used to hammer us hard saying that we had to make an IPA. So, we made an IPA with *Brettanomyces* yeast called Phrenology. I'll stand behind that beer forever because it got picked the eleventh-best IPA in the country by *Paste* magazine out of four hundred IPAs. I feel great about that, but it didn't sell for shit. So, we quit making it, and our distributor said we had to make another IPA. So, we made a sour IPA, and it didn't sell for shit. Then we just said, "Fuck it, we're not listening to you." This is a sour brewery. I don't think it's radically different from what Blank Slate went through...

MIKE: Although, he's been a little more willing to change.

SCOTT: I was completely unwilling to change.

BRET: Well, I probably wouldn't have been if I didn't have two other business partners hammering me all the time early on.

SCOTT: That probably would have helped me. I was running unfettered. There was nobody telling me this is a good idea or this is a bad idea. It was just, "This is what we're doing," and everybody would say, "OK."

BRET: Well, I resented the shit out of them at the time, but I'm thankful. Now, I like change, but I hold values.

SCOTT: Going back to your stupid things people would say. At festivals, I would have Shroominess, a beer made with mushrooms, on tap. People would always say, "Oh, is it magic mushrooms?" So, I'd give them some, and I really wouldn't say anything. They'd taste it, and they'd say, "Oh, yeah, that's pretty good." Then, I'd be like, "Yeah, you like it?" "Yeah." "Cool. You've got twenty minutes to get some place safe." And they'd go, "What?!" "No, I'm fucking with you, man." We're not putting illegal drugs in our beer! Although, we talked about doing it someday, making like a six barrel with actual magic mushrooms, just invite friends and family, and have a lock-in event.

MIKE: Could you still do that, and can I get some?

SCOTT: It never got super far. I don't know. I'd have to look into how you could brew it and still have the effects.

BRET: I'm sure it can be done. Let's try it.

SCOTT: I would start trying to dry hop it with the shrooms, but I don't know if you'd get enough extraction by doing that. If you cook it, denature it?

BRET: Could you put them in the fermenter?

SCOTT: I don't know. It warrants more research.

❖ ❖ ❖

The brilliance of Scott LaFollette is in this very moment. A joke, taken to the point of hypothetical reality. Examining in detail what it would take to create something that has never been done. This is creativity in action. As ludicrous as something like magic mushroom beer is, by going through the exercise of making it a reality, practical ideas can present themselves. This is what we always loved about Blank Slate, the ability to turn a ridiculous idea into a delicious reality.

❖ ❖ ❖

BRET: What was your happiest moment in craft beer?

SCOTT: Damn. Probably the one-year anniversary party at Blank Slate. We did a whole day thing. It wasn't huge, but it was a big event for us. I had just taken over the next-door space in the building to put in more fermentation and start canning, but I hadn't built it out. It was a big, empty room. So, we had an anniversary party. We had the bar and two different serving stations. We got some bands. We did a bunch of special keg spikes and infusions and stuff, and every hour we tapped a new beer. We debuted a few new beers, and Opera Cream Stout was coming back out for the season or whatever. We'd done a bunch of planning. I had a super small staff, and they were all fucking awesome. We got some volunteers, and everything went off without a hitch. Everyone had a good time. After that night was over and everything was done and cleaned up, about one in the morning, the staff and I hung out for a while. Then they all went home, and I sat down at the bar. All the lights were off. It was dark. It was quiet. I had just had this amazing day, and I sat there and drank a beer by myself. That was when I thought, "We're really going to do something here. We're on the up and up." Money wasn't good, but we were solving it. I thought, "We're going to grow. We're going to do this." I felt like we had this great runway in front of us, and we had this super awesome thing. That was probably my favorite moment in all my life in craft beer.

MIKE: That sounds like a very nice moment in time.

SCOTT: Yeah, and then it just all went down from there. I still get a little emotional about it. It's why I don't talk about Blank Slate a lot.

MIKE: You should get emotional about it, Scott, because you put heart and soul into that place. It was your own creation. You literally built most of it with your bare hands, and I think that was a big, sad part of the problem. In *Brew Skies Happy Hour* podcast, we spend a lot of time talking about capital. It's always very cynical, and it also always comes down to one thing: the people with the money always win.

SCOTT: Oh, yeah, absolutely—until they decide that they don't want to do it anymore. It's not easy enough, so they get bored and pull the plug.

MIKE: You're such a great example of the other side of that coin. In the 2010s, I think you were making the best beer in the city. Blank Slate's reputation was unquestionable. The beer was brilliant, but you started out with a brewery that you built from scratch in your spare time with the money that you could put aside, and you were never well-capitalized. Then, a brewery called Streetside opened roughly a block away. It was, in my opinion, a vastly inferior brewery, although it was well-capitalized. Today, you're gone and it's doing great. There's a brewery across the street from Urban Artifact called Humble Monk. When they were planning on opening, I know that it drove Bret crazy that somebody was going to open a brewery across the street from his brewery, but I don't think that it has hurt Urban Artifact at all. They make completely different styles, and businesses like bars and breweries sometimes profit from competition because they become an area with options rather than an island. The net effect of competition becomes more customers for everybody. What effect did Streetside have on Blank Slate? Did they help or hurt?

SCOTT: I know one of the owners, and he was always a super nice guy. And in those days, we were nowhere near a point of saturation. There was the idea that a rising tide raises all boats. We had even been talking about having the East End pub crawl or taproom crawl. There were three taprooms in the East End—Blank Slate, Streetside and Bad Tom Smith——which was kind of weird and I would argue not a good idea, but that was how it was. I've always been a glass-half-empty guy, unfortunately. So, I was a little leery, a little scared, but there was nothing I could do about it. The annoying thing was that the guys who started Streetside used to be in my place all the time. They were some of my best customers. So, when they opened their own place, I lost some of my best customers. They were always asking questions, and I was always very, very helpful. I don't regret any of that. But I think with Humble Monk and Urban Artifact, both located in Northside, there are areas where it works because you can hit two or three places. Otherwise, some people might not come to either brewery. But there are scenarios where it doesn't work as well. We were in that second scenario. It was way more industrial. The location is more car-centric. I could walk to Streetside, obviously. It was literally a stone's throw away, but a couple of things made it different from Urban Artifact and Humble Monk. Number one, they built a brand-new building, and I was in a shitty fucking warehouse. Also, we were not on a main thoroughfare. You had to cut down what's basically an alley to get to our place, cross railroad tracks past a dive bar. Not that many people drive on that cut-through street. You had to know where you were going. No one came down that street and was like, "Oh, there's a brewery here!" You only went down the street because you were coming to Blank Slate. Streetside being so close but not on the same street didn't have a positive effect. They had way better street frontage, and it was way easier to find. There was more street parking than at my place, and it was a nice, pretty, new building, with better scenery. All those things were a contributing factor. The day they opened, my taproom sales went down 30 percent and never recovered.

MIKE: Jesus Christ!

SCOTT: I haven't told a lot of people that. I can't say it was because they opened, but it's a very interesting coincidence. I do not want to say that there's direct causation there, but I will say there's definitely a correlation. I don't blame them.

BRET: They weren't coming for your number.

SCOTT: I'd like to believe they weren't. Maybe they were. I don't know, but I don't think about it that way. We talked a lot about how it'll be cool. People can come down and hit both of our places, and it becomes more of a destination. It might have been great if I wasn't in such a shitty building, with such shitty parking, on a shitty street, next to the fucking sewer plant.

BRET: Well, that wasn't something that you had to think about in the beginning. Being a retail space wasn't part of your mindset. It wasn't even legal when you started working on Blank Slate. The breweries that had been opening at that time were purely production.

SCOTT: Yeah, right. Blank Slate wasn't my first stab at things. I was involved in a project that never got anywhere that was going to be a brewpub. I always thought the ultimate thing would be to have a brewpub. I always thought that fit more with what I wanted to do, what I wanted to be, but I didn't know anything about food, didn't have the ability to even figure that out. In those days, because I funded the thing myself, I could barely put together a brewery in a shitty warehouse in a terrible part of town. I couldn't build a restaurant, but the hope was that maybe someday we would spin off a brewpub. To this day, honestly, the ultimate thing for me would be to have a

Blank Slate's draft board on the last day of operation in August 2017. *Courtesy of Scott LaFollette.*

brewpub and be able to run the beer side. If I could do a thousand barrels out of my own space with a restaurant attached—profitably—that's all I'd ever need. But I was one of the last breweries that were approved in the state of Ohio before the taproom law passed [which made it feasible for breweries to have taprooms].

MIKE: That's just bad luck.

SCOTT: I had heard they were trying to get that legislation through. I got my license, it was another month before I was able to brew and another month or so before anything started going out the door. It was in that two-month time frame that the law changed. I remember very distinctly; my wife and I were at a concert down at Taft. It was intermission, and I was at the cheesy little cash bar getting a beer. And I pulled out my phone and saw this news article about how they had just approved taprooms in Ohio. I was like, "What the fuck?!" I thought, "I can't do anything about this, I'm too far in." So, I didn't worry about it too much. People look back at it now and ask,

"Why the hell didn't you shift into that model?" Well, I was way too deep. Also, there were a lot of guys at the time that were like, "Why would I want to do that? I make beer. I don't run a bar. I don't know how to run a bar, and who's going to want to come to my brewery in a random warehouse in the middle of nowhere and sit at a bar that I'm going to make out of two-by-fours and busted old pallets?" We didn't know how it was going to work out. In those days, pre-taproom law, you needed three things to start a brewery in this town: cheap rent, high ceilings and a loading dock. Those were literally the only three things I was looking for because it was only meant to be for production. No one was ever coming there. Look at MadTree's first location. It was 100 percent those three things. They were building it to be production only, but they were early enough in their build-out, because they didn't come along until about a year after Blank Slate, that they had enough time to pivot and jam in a little taproom. It felt cobbled together, but it worked because they still had a bigger space than me.

MIKE: They built that original taproom for less than $10,000.

SCOTT: Correct, but people wouldn't go for that today.

BRET: Looking back, you could have validly seen your space, or MadTree's original location or even Rhinegeist and wondered why anybody would think they would work as a retail space.

SCOTT: I have a good Rhinegeist story. Guess what I said to Bryant and Bob [owners and founders of Rhinegeist Brewery] before they opened? I said, "You're crazy. You're insane. No one is going to come to this fucking place. There are hookers on your front porch." And this is the coup de grâce of how stupid I am. They said that they were going to can. I was like, "Why are you going to can? Nobody cans. People think canned beer is cheap beer." That was like a year before they opened. They said, "Well, they're going to have this streetcar line go past here." I said, "Dude, they're never going to build that thing. Are you stupid?"

MIKE: Without the benefit of hindsight, those were all legitimate viewpoints then.

SCOTT: Well, I don't know how legitimate it was, but definitely more legitimate back then than it sounds now. I didn't have the vision that they had. I was like, "Why are you putting the brewery on the second floor? Put it in the basement. Are you stupid?" Literally everything they did, I told them, "You guys are fucking idiots."

MIKE: Rhinegeist played every card right, but they're a perfect example of what being well-capitalized does for you.

SCOTT: Oh, absolutely, and they had the right people with the right experience, especially for this town. Nobody knew how to sell beer like they did.

BRET: I know the struggles that we had as a sour brewery in 2015. What was it like in the earliest days of Blank Slate trying to explain to Cincinnatians that beer made with mushrooms is still beer? Beer doesn't have to be yellow and fizzy.

SCOTT: I can go one step more basic than that. When I started, it was just draft, and I was self-distributing. So, I'm going around to bars that were craft friendly, whatever the hell we even thought that meant at the time, and I would get so many weird responses. The biggest one was, "I can't buy it from you. You can't sell it to me yourself. You're not a distributor." I literally had to print out the part of the section of the Ohio Revised Code about self-distribution. I had to carry that around with me and show it to bar managers, who, of course, didn't want to read it. I had to sometimes argue with beer buyers that yes, indeed, they could buy beer from me. It was legal. It was OK. I didn't just make this in my bathtub. Now, I'm telling you to buy it from me. Probably 50 percent of the places I went, I had to have that discussion. Then there were places I walked into that were always like, "Well, you know, my Corona rep usually gets me Reds tickets or Bengals tickets. So, if you've got something like that, we'll put you on tap."

MIKE: You were so early in the craft beer scene in this city, did you also have trouble with bureaucrats not understanding small, production breweries?

SCOTT: Yeah, there was definitely some of that. Most of the issues that I ran into were dealing with the city, but the one that really got me was the freaking FDA came in.

BRET: What? The FDA? They don't have jurisdiction, not at that scale.

SCOTT: Yeah, technically you are a food manufacturing facility, but they don't normally fuck with breweries. It was literally just a roll of the dice, bad luck of the draw. Somebody told somebody that they needed to go inspect a brewery. They probably opened the phone book, and guess what the first one in the phone book was? It started with a B. I don't know. But they showed up one day, and this was even before we had the taproom, and they just raked me over the coals. My lights weren't bright enough. "How can you clean your vessels if the lights aren't bright enough to see in there?" I'm like, "They're cleaned in place internally. I can put the light of the Sun above this tank, and I'm still not going to be able to clean inside of it any better. It doesn't matter what the ambient light is—it's how bright of a light I can shine into it when I open it." I didn't have the proper covers on my fluorescent light fixtures, and they weren't the proper color. But the biggest one was, because it was a warehouse and it had big garage doors, the garage doors were always open. You can't keep them open because of bugs and shit, but we had been operating for a while and we'd never had any problems. And I shit you not, it's the only day it ever happened in the history of that facility, but a bird flew in that day. The brewery had peaked roofs, so it took the bird a while to figure out how to get out. That's when the FDA came, and there's a bird flying around. They were like, "You absolutely, 100 percent can't have open doors." "Well, I can't close these doors because I'll suffocate." At that time, all my refrigeration equipment was inside. I came in one morning around seven in the morning in August, and the thermometer I had right inside the doors read 116 degrees. It was like walking into a furnace. I couldn't just close the doors. So, I'm the smallest little guy in town, barely making it, barely making a living, and I had to go out and spend $8,000 on roll-up screen doors for my garage doors. Then, for however many years after that, every brewery that opened had huge garage doors that were open all the time. I was just like, goddammit!

BRET: What's the craziest beer idea you ever had? And did you end up doing it?

SCOTT: Absolutely, I did it. To this day, it's the most amazing thing I feel like I was ever involved in creating. I got a bourbon barrel that had been used to age hot sauce. We put a black saison in a hot sauce barrel. When that beer was done, it was the most amazingly interesting mix of flavors I've ever had in a beer. The fact that it was blacked didn't really matter. It wasn't chocolatey or roasty, but it probably helped hide whatever weird color was extracted from the barrel. The saison character was really dry, and it had this beautiful mixture of heat with a vinegar bite in the back because it was a vinegar-based hot sauce. We called it Spectral Fire, which is a line from a Mars Volta song a long time ago. It was probably the second-most polarizing beer I ever made. You either loved it or you hated it, and I was cool with that.

BRET: What was the most polarizing?

SCOTT: The alcoholic kombucha experiments.

BRET: I talked to Mike about that before you got here. I was remembering those kombucha-beer hybrids. They were crazy!

SCOTT: I had not done nearly enough research on the proper ways to make kombucha, all the balances. It came out really acidic, like enamel-scraping acidic. I made it in an old tank. No temperature control, which ended up being its downfall. I didn't have a way to jacket the tank or anything, so it was fermenting at like eighty-five degrees, which made it jarringly acidic. You either loved it or you hated it, and I wasn't sure which side of that fence I was even on, but it was interesting. It was something fun to try for a while, but I gave it up. It was pretty cool, but yeah, very polarizing.

❖ ❖ ❖

Blank Slate was a true brewery iconoclast. Traditional beer was not sacred to Scott. You cannot move forward, grow, evolve and become your best brewery if you hold true to the way things have always been done. Innovation was not a line item in Blank Slate's business plan—it *was* its business. Its avant-garde spirit brought it infamy. It's why it's still revered to this day. It's why its impact on the brewing scene in Cincinnati, while tragically short, is legendary.

SERVING CINCINNATI'S FIRST CRAFT BEER

Jim Tarbell and Jack

JIM TARBELL

Jim Tarbell's moniker is "Mr. Cincinnati," and in 2016 he was immortalized in a four-story mural on Vine Street. So, of course he helped shaped the Cincinnati beer scene. He has lived life full of adventures and on his own terms. He served on Cincinnati City Council from 1999 to 2005 for the maximum number of years and was appointed vice-mayor, a power that he once used to override the city manager's decision to cancel the annual Bockfest Parade, personally leading it through a blizzard. (We won't mince the legality of his actual authority.) He has owned two bars and a music venue that his force of personality made legendary in each instance. This includes Arnold's Bar & Grill, where he presided over the tapping of Cincinnati's first craft beer at in 1981.

◆ ◆ ◆

MIKE: You've owned several bars and helped shape some of the beer scene in this city in different ways. Do you remember what your first beers were personally?

JIM: I was coming of age at sixteen with "the cadre," this group that hung out together in high school. We had our driver's licenses, some of us, and that was the license to steal or get into lots of trouble. One or the other—or both. In this case, it led us to Over-the-Rhine and all the hillbilly—I say this respectfully—all the hillbilly bars on Vine Street. Some were off of Vine, but most of them were on Vine. There was country then, rockabilly and rhythm-and-blues. Roland Kirk was early on in his career. He was living in Columbus, and he used to come down here on the weekends and play with this R&B band at the Swing Bar, at the corner of Thirteenth Street. You could get served there—all these places—as long as you weren't an idiot, you know, as long as you had cash and you could keep your mouth shut. But in the case of the Swing Bar, they had Hudepohl on tap. You could get a glass of Hudepohl, free admission and then a fight, guaranteed. You'd see the bartender on a regular basis come from behind the bar with a baseball bat to break up a fight. So, you had a glass of Hudepohl, free music and a fight for twenty-five cents. [Rahsaan Roland Kirk was a blind saxophonist the *Columbus Monthly* called the "most consequential musical genius ever to come out of Columbus." He played with Jimi Hendrix, Thelonious Monk and John Coltrane, among others.]

BRET: That sounds like a great deal.

JIM: What's not to like about that? It was 1958, and Vine Street was the be-all-and-end-all for adult entertainment, or for teenagers making their transition to adults. When we went to Vine Street, it was all male. We left the girls behind, except for Sonny Starling. She went to Ursuline, but she lived downtown, above the Blue Note Café. Her father bartended at the Arrow Café, on Thirteenth Street and Clay. It was just a fun, neighborhood bar, and her father was a bartender, so we went there automatically because we could get served under his sponsorship. I have to tell this story about the Arrow Café, though. All these places were kind of rough. Over-the-Rhine people were moving out to the suburbs or wherever, and the neighborhood was filled with blue-collar guys, mostly from Appalachia, who came to Cincinnati to get jobs at GE and the Ford factory in Evandale. But they came to Over-the-Rhine because that's where the music was, and they wanted to hear some music when they got off of work and were drinking beer, and there were several places that always had music. We'd always start at the Arrow Café, but the first time we went into the Arrow, a guy had ripped the pay phone off the wall, and he was beating this guy with it, on the ground, you know.

The "Court Street Irregulars," Jim Tarbell's band of merry urban-dwelling friends in the early 1970s. The bearded mountain man in the center is Jim. *Courtesy of Jim Tarbell, Chris Breeden and Arnold's Bar & Grill.*

Then there was kind of a break in the action, and I was sitting at the bar next to the girlfriend of this guy, R.B. was his name, a real beat-'em-up guy. When it was time for us to leave, I thought I needed to help somehow. I've just got to help her out. She looks innocent, you know. So, I leaned over on my way out, and I said, "You know, you need to get away from this guy—he's dangerous." Well, he heard everything I said, but by the time it registered with him, telepathically, I was past him. My friend Pat was the next in line, so he swung at Pat, thinking he was me. Pat ducked, and he hit Steve. So, there were three of us involved in that punch.

We'd go to Vine Street for these reasons. There was Pappy's, the Silver Dollar, Swing Bar. There were bars all over the place, but seven or eight of them had live music. So, it was a great place to hang out, and that's sort of my first venture into social drinking, and it was usually Hudepohl.

◆ ◆ ◆

When you ask Jim Tarbell for a story, you always get a good one, but it's long and circuitous. So, we'll summarize just a few of the things that happened between Jim developing an appreciation for local beer on Vine Street in the late 1950s and purchasing Arnold's in 1976. He got a job at a hospital delivering plants to patients. Visibly bored and not afraid of blood, he worked his way up to being a surgical assistant in operating theaters. While working in Clifton hospitals, he discovered Joey's Delicatessen & Liquor Store, an overlooked legend for having a surprisingly good beer selection decades before carrying imported and craft beers became commonplace, and it was revolutionary when Tarbell was in his late teens. Here, he was introduced to "exotic" imports. He couldn't afford them all the time, but he started buying

A young Jim Tarbell playing the trombone outside Arnold's Bar & Grill, something that he used to do to drum up business in the early days before the bar became the epicenter of downtown nightlife. We assume that when Jim lured a potential customer with his siren song, the beagle chased the mark down. *Courtesy of Jim Tarbell, Chris Breeden and Arnold's Bar & Grill.*

them periodically to expand his palate, even collecting bottles of his favorites on "a little altar." Jim wanted to become a doctor, but he's dyslexic, a condition that wasn't understood in that era, and it caused a professor to crush his dreams. So, he took the logical next career step: he became a cook on a North Atlantic fishing boat out of Gloucester, Massachusetts.

His father died tragically and unexpectedly young, so Jim returned to Cincinnati for a while. His travel lust unsated, he decided to go out to the San Francisco Bay area in the late '60s. Yes, we're talking about the height of the whole free love hippie movement that defines the collective image and stereotype of the 1960s, and Jim was a particularly adroit tourist of the scene. He spent time hanging out with Owsley Stanley, the "King of Acid"; Ken Kesey; and the rest of the Merry Pranksters. As Mike sat slack-jawed in wonder at this part of the story, Bret said, "I swear to God, I think you guys are just making a bunch of shit up." So, if you're under a certain age and these names sound like gibberish, look it up on your stupid little phone.

Then, Jim came back to Cincinnati and decided to open a music venue called Ludlow Garage. Booking up-and-coming acts that included Carlos Santana, the Allman Brothers, Neil Young and Alice Cooper turned the Ludlow Garage into Cincinnati musical legend, but it didn't last very long as a business venture. Jim bumped around for a while, ran a thrift shop and then decided to buy a run-down dive named Arnold's Bar & Grill because he needed a place for his friends to hang out, which takes us back to the question that we asked more than an hour earlier.

◆ ◆ ◆

MIKE: You bought Arnold's, and you redefined what it was, partly by being the only serious live music bar downtown, partly because of legendarily good food and eventually because Arnold's featured some of the first craft and imported beers on draft in the city. Was better beer always part of that vision, because you'd developed the knowledge that there was good beer out there?

JIM: Well, traveling was a big part of it. I was on other continents, Europe.

MIKE: What was the first craft or import that you served at Arnold's, and how did people respond to it?

JIM: Well, I wasn't shy about marketing, and all these things about Arnold's history played right into my hands, this new old place, what it's been about historically and why it's important. What we put on the plate, or in the bottle, or in the glass or on stage—those were all important, but some things just had to be resurrected. That was the gift of buying the business in the first place, what it came with, then a lot of the rest was just adding some imagination to the history and the physical things that were already there. It was such a perfect package for crazy people like me. Now, to answer your question, Christian Moerlein was first. I can't give you dates, but I know that I was so excited about it. The first keg of Moerlein was brought by a team of horses to Arnold's. It was huge. Two horses, two drivers and I think they had two kegs.

BRET: What I've learned from the Amish, if anything, is that drinking and driving doesn't apply to horse-drawn carriages.

MIKE: That's terrible legal advice, but sure. Was Arnold's also the first bar in Cincinnati to serve Guinness?

JIM: Yeah. There were some challenges there because there's a special way to deliver Guinness, and nobody knew how to sell Guinness in Cincinnati, except me, and I said that we couldn't do it because you had to pour it with nitrogen. It's a different system. You could get nitrous oxide in a tank, but you had to have a special coupling unit…

BRET: Not straight nitrogen? You wanted to serve Guinness on laughing gas?!

JIM: Yeah.

BRET: That's probably why it did so well. Get a little high, get a little drunk.

JIM: That hardly ever came up. It was all about getting the nitrous oxide and getting the distributor up to speed with how it all worked. I ended up going to the Dubliner Pub in Washington, D.C., and the guy there was tickled to be able to help me figure it all out, how you deliver it best.

BRET: How did you even get your distributor to carry Guinness? If you were the only place in the city to get it, no one was even selling it.

JIM: Oh, well, you had to be Tarbell. Don't give up, you know, don't give up. You didn't know how much fun all this was. Some things I carry with me; I miss Arnold's every day.

◆ ◆ ◆

In 1999, Jim was serving on city council, and he had also opened an ambitious new venture called Grammer's, a spectacularly intact turn-of-the-last-century German restaurant and saloon in north Over-the-Rhine, which was challenged by being too far ahead of its time. He thought that he was stretched too thin, so he sold Arnold's to his longtime manager, Ronda Breeden. Ronda sold the business to her son, Chirs Breeden, immediately before COVID hit (sorry, Chris), and the Breedens have proven good stewards of keeping the soul of "Cincinnati's oldest continuously operating bar" alive.

Tarbell in his traditional court jester costume in the Bockfest Parade. Behind him, Keith Baker and the Bockfest Monks pull the Trojan Goat. *Courtesy of Alex Bell.*

◆ ◆ ◆

Jack: Cincinnati's Bartender

If Tarbell is "Mr. Cincinnati," Mike Toebbe should forever been known as "Cincinnati's Bartender." Almost nobody, however, knows who the hell Mike Toebbe is, partly because the city knew him as Jack. His ultra-laid-back persona also didn't result in a lot of nominations for any of the "best of" lists that give bartenders regional fame. In a career behind the bar at Arnold's that stretched from 1978 to 2020, Jack stayed Jack. Old-school. He'd just as soon take a kick in the nads as make a fruity cocktail, and if anybody ever suggested that he start rendering his own simple syrup, he would have contemplated a response and then walked the other way. His primary skills during more than forty years behind the bar are endangered these days, the art of conversation and telling mildly off-color jokes—along with a remarkable ability to wing an eight-ounce bottle of beer across the room. Jack also holds the distinction of tapping Cincinnati's first craft beer in 1981. Mike Morgan and Jack had hundreds of conversations over decades of Fridays, most of them fuzzy, but the following occurred in a booth at Arnold's with a tape recorder capturing it, back in the pre-COVID world.

◆ ◆ ◆

MIKE: Jim Tarbell made Arnold's Bar & Grill an institution in Cincinnati, and you've been there since almost the beginning of that era. When did you become a bartender at Arnold's?

JACK: 1978. Tarbell bought it in '76.

MIKE: How did you wind up there? Were you already in the business?

JACK: I was an unemployed drunk. Scott Ebert was a bartender there at the time. He says, "Man, you need a job. Why don't you go to Arnold's and tell Tarbell you want my job." I said, "I can't do that." He says, "Just go to Arnold's and say that you need a job. Say, 'I'll do anything. I don't care what it is.'" So, I went, and Tarbell says, "Well, we don't have any bartender jobs, but we do need a barback." I said, "Okay." He says, "You know what that is?" I'm going, "Yeah, I think so." He says, "Just stocking, move a bunch of shit up from our basement." I'm like, "I can handle that." Ebert asks, "When can you start? How about tonight?" This is on a Thursday, and I'm going, "Wait a minute, I was thinking, like, two weeks from now." I said, "I can't do it tonight." So, he says, "How about tomorrow night? It's Friday night." Ebert wants me to have his job, so I say, "Okay."

MIKE: Why did he want you to take his job?

JACK: He loved Arnold's, but he'd helped build a bar in Covington and he wanted to work there, but he didn't want to leave Tarbell stranded. I got here at 5:30. It was the first hot day of the year. So, I go down to the basement and pulled up these old big-ass fans and plug them in. Fan didn't work. So, I took the housing off of it, tightened it up, put it back together and it worked. Tarbell says, "Man, that's great!" I'm going, "Yeah. I've only been working here for half an hour and I've already fixed your air conditioning system." So, it came time for Ebert to come in. He just didn't come in. And so, there's me, who's never been behind a bar in my life.

MIKE: That's how you worked your way up to being a bartender at Arnold's? A conspiracy against Tarbell?

JACK: Yeah. Back in those days, it was packed. Always packed. Always. We didn't even have tape in the register. It wasn't like today. It was an open register, and you wrote shit down.

MIKE: I used to tend bar in a place with an open register. It was lucrative for me, but not in a particularly honest way.

JACK: Well, Jim had a sense that I was pretty honest. He knew that I was an honest guy, I wouldn't try to screw anybody out of anything. So, after two or three weeks, I was running a register. Arnold's was the hottest bar in town. Especially Friday nights—it was huge.

MIKE: What made the place so hot back then?

JACK: Oh, it was like a multipurpose bar. Everybody is welcome. Prices were super cheap. So, like, bums could come in. At a basic happy hour, you'd have moms, lawyers, business executives, elbow to elbow. Beer was forty-five cents. Mixed drinks were like seventy-five cents. Bums could afford it. Rich people thought it was the coolest. It was just a great blast.

MIKE: That was still part of the feeling when I started going there in 1999. You could get a pitcher of Christian Moerlein for around five bucks.

JACK: Oh yeah, super cheap. When I started working there, we sold so much of their beer that Hudepohl built a four-tap system and a walk-in box for free. We only used two taps out of the four, and they were Hudepohl and Hudepohl. You just used one. Then, when you ran out, you didn't have to go change anything. It was great, because I weighed like 170 pounds when I started working there, and those barrels were like 330 pounds—double me, and I couldn't push them around. They built all that shit for us. That's what breweries did back in those days.

It looked nothing like it does now. I think it was like '79, and Jim found this bar in Covington in a bar that closed, and it fit Arnold's perfectly. The bar was twenty-six feet long, and it was one piece of wood. It still is. We put in hardwood floors behind the bar and then put that bar in. Everything behind the bar was so rotten that you'd fall through it when I first started working there.

MIKE: Arnold's has changed as downtown has evolved, and a lot of the clientele has changed with it. I remember what it was like in the early 2000s. I'm sure that the crowd was a hell of a lot different in the '80s.

JACK: What drove a lot of it back then was artists and shit. Poets from Mount Adams, hippies that started growing up. It was super cheap, so like a whole shit load of artists and poets of every kind gravitated towards Arnold's. It was kind of cool, and a lot of people knew Tarbell. Plus, a lot of those guys lived downtown. We had a bunch of semi-ex-hippies, semi-hippies, that kind of thing.

MIKE: What was the waitstaff like when you started working there? Did you work with some of the longtime employees that Tarbell inherited when he bought it? I've heard they were pretty colorful.

JACK: Yeah, Sadie and Mary. Sadie had been working there for twenty years, and Mary worked there for nineteen. Those girls were freaking awesome. Sadie was super irreverent. She'd say shit like, "I'm so hungry I could eat the asshole out of a skunk." When my wife started working days there, she said there were some business people sitting in the booth, taking a business lunch. They've got their papers out. We were like really busy. Sadie stands right next to the table, and she says, "Would you look at these suits sitting there in this booth finger fucking? Don't they know I need this table?" They were like, "I guess we're done." They got up and left. They weren't pissed or anything because that's the way it was. She and Mary. They were two of a kind. You never knew what was going to come out of their mouth. It could be anything.

MIKE: You and Billy Cunningham became a pretty famous duo in town for a spectacle called "the Little Kings toss." When did you start working together?

JACK: Probably '80, but I can't remember.

MIKE: When did you guys start doing the Little Kings toss?

JACK: Early in the '80s sometime.

MIKE: Was it something you did every night that you guys worked together?

JACK: Oh yeah. As a matter of fact, Amy Culbertson, who was a regular, wrote the entertainment section for the *Post*. She would cover Arnold's like, Monday, the Good Time Jazz Band; Tuesday, Katie Lauer; blah, blah, blah; Friday, some band; and of course, "Jack and Billy and the Amazing Beer Bottle Toss." It ran in the paper like that every week.

❖ ❖ ❖

Explanatory Note: Jack and Billy always worked the bar on Friday nights. When someone ordered a Little Kings Cream Ale from the opposite end of the bar from where it was stocked in the cooler, the Amazing Beer Bottle Toss consisted of one of these guys throwing an open bottle of it hurtling through the air to the other to serve to the customer—in a packed bar.

❖ ❖ ❖

From left to right: Jack, Billy Cunningham, an as-yet-unidentified bartender and Blair, posing behind Arnold's bar with a Guinness tap in the early 1980s. *Courtesy of Chris Breeden, Arnold's Bar & Grill.*

JACK: We did probably the all-time world's record beer bottle toss. We were getting pretty damn good at it. Billy had really good hands, and I threw this perfect spiral.

MIKE: How do you throw an open beer without spilling any of it?

JACK: The way to throw a Little Kings is to spin it, like a football. When it came off my fingers, it would rotate, kind of a gyroscope thing. We did one where I was down at the very front of the bar by the front door. We were going for the world's record. We had a barback at the door to the next room holding people back, so people couldn't walk into it if something bad happened. I threw this Little Kings bottle from the front of the building, like in front of the bar. We moved the tables out of the way back to the kitchen, and Billy's waiting for this thing. You've got to throw it pretty damn high. So, it was almost up to the ceiling, but not quite. When it went across the end of the bar by the door to the next room, it was straight up and down. It was perfect. Then it started going around and around, and Billy grabbed it and caught it in one motion.

MIKE: That's a long ass way to throw an open beer.

JACK: Oh yeah, just the bar is twenty-six feet long. There was a regular customer named Bonnie, and Billy hands it over to her, and she says, "That's bullshit. I paid for a full beer. That's not a full beer. There's some running out the end." Because some foam came out, she wanted another one. Like, uh, okay. Billy is standing at the end of the bar, so I reach into the cooler, grab one off the top and throw it. Billy catches it and puts it in front of her, and nothing runs out. It was awesome.

MIKE: You just can't do that stuff now.

JACK: We were drunk.

MIKE: Didn't you tell me once that Arnold's was the number one Little Kings account in the city and that it lost that status when you stopped drinking?

JACK: Well, I always drank Little Kings when I worked 'cause, you know, seven ounces, down the hatch. Stays cold. And then we had a lot of customers that would see me drinking them and having a good time, so they'd drink Little Kings too. So, when I quit drinking in like 1987, the Hudepohl beer salesman (who also sold Little Kings) said, "Jack, you son of a bitch, when you were drinking, we sold four cases of Little Kings at Arnold's a week. Now we sell like one case a month." I go, "Sorry about that." Of course, I worked every day back in those days.

MIKE: When did you stop tending bar full-time?

JACK: Beats me. I really don't know.

❖ ❖ ❖

That's partly because it was a gradual thing. Jack got a call from his mom one day, saying that his dad was working himself to death in his machine shop. He needed help. Jack didn't want to work in a machine shop, but he loved and listened to his mom. For example, Jack only got his hair cut once a year, right before Mother's Day, as a gift. So, he started going to work in the shop at 7:30 every morning, working a full day, and then tending bar at Arnold's. Eventually, the bartending shifts decreased until Jack primarily became the Friday night bartender, occasionally taking naps in a booth before his shift started.

Jack and Billy continued to work together until Billy moved to Grammer's, Tarbell's new bar in 1992. Until then, the Jack & Billy Show, as it was referred to in *Cincinnati* magazine in the '80s, continued to hone a low-boil routine. They fell into a role, with Jack always playing the straight man. Sometimes they were assisted by things that Billy bought at a magic supplies store: fake quarters and rigged cigarettes that made George Washington smoke, for example. Sometimes it was just corny jokes delivered deadpan. For example:

❖ ❖ ❖

BILLY *(fumbling with something)*: I'm getting worried about my eyes, Jack. I've been seeing spots.

JACK: That's bad, Billy, have you seen an eye doctor?

BILLY *(contemplative)*: No, just the spots.

❖ ❖ ❖

"We had a lot of fun and made a lot of money," Jack says. "He got my shit." We talked about some of the most famous and infamous former regulars and semi-regulars, including one of Cincinnati's mayors with a reputation for inebriation and another former mayor with a reputation for a certain infamous talk show among other things.

❖ ❖ ❖

MIKE: Jerry Springer used to be regular, right?

JACK: For a while, he was a regular. We had a girl that was a barback that was, like, nuclear. [This means extremely attractive.] She was like eighteen years old, and Jerry had it bad for her. That was back right after his troubles with the hooker. [As mayor, Springer was in a scandal involving a brothel in Covington.] Yeah, he had it bad, and he would come in like a dog sniffing another dog.

MIKE: Did he succeed?

JACK: Oh, yeah. She got fired for that shit. I always tell friends about people that came in that were semi-famous, but I never really think about Jerry Springer as being one of them. I guess he is but, you know, Jerry used to call me. For a while, he came in every Friday.

◆ ◆ ◆

Arnold's has served so many semi-famous and very famous people by now that they're too numerous to list. Among the longtime staff, George Wendt comes up a lot as a favorite experience. Wendt, who played Norm in *Cheers*, sat at the bar for hours, good-naturedly tossing back beers and talking to other barflies just like his TV character, reportedly leaving hammered.

As we put down a few more beers, Jack and I talked about how working at Arnold's has changed over the years. For one thing, the flow of the traffic has changed. Tending bar evolved into being more restaurant focused. "It's real busy at lunch time," he explains, "so a lot of folks serve a lot of folks." Referring to a predominantly female daytime staff, he says, "When the rush is gone, we all sit around the table at the end of the bar. We talk about periods and shopping."

◆ ◆ ◆

MIKE: What things have changed the most?

JACK: The vibe. For one thing, we've got all these goofy drinks, so we need three bartenders to make all these goofy drinks. Two people would be swamped by all these goofy drinks. When we were a kick-ass bar, we had two bartenders, we'd kick ass, and we were happy serving beers and wine. Now, we need three bartenders and a barback because you can't make all those goofy drinks in a timely fashion and serve everybody. So, the bartenders make less money. I make way less money now than I did like three or four years ago 'cause I gotta split it three and a half ways, but the bar makes a lot more money. These drinks make like 99 percent profit. There's a special drink list. They all suck 'cause I hate to make them. I don't feel right about it, for Arnold's being a 150-year-old bar making these fucking poofy *Sex in the City* cocktails. I'm pretty sure it's not right. Arnold's wasn't founded on these principles. When I started working here, it was a kick-ass bar for the one reason: it was simple. Simple, cheap, simple, good. Now there's not even a discussion. I say, "I think this sucks." They're like, "You know how much money we make off these?" "Well, yeah, I do." "Well, then shut the fuck up." It's not nearly as enjoyable, and now I'm broke. I don't know, but I couldn't imagine sitting at home on a Friday night knowing I could be at Arnold's instead. Can you imagine that? After all these years? Sitting there watching TV? I couldn't do that. I gotta be at Arnold's, even if I don't make any money. You know, it's what I do. It's my thing.

MIKE: Personally, I can't imagine you not doing it. You're the last real authentic link to the old days.

JACK: Oh, yeah. As a matter of fact, I think Ronda knows that. I think Chris knows that [referencing Ronda Breeden, who purchased Arnold's in 1999 from Jim Tarbell, and her son and heir apparent, Chris Breeden, who bought the bar from his mom in 2020]. That's probably the only reason I'm there, why they don't fuck with me at all. Although, they do a little bit. When they stopped letting bartenders drink, stuff like that.

MIKE: Aren't you the only one still allowed to drink?

JACK: Well, it used to be, "Nobody can drink except Jack." Then that turned into nobody, and that really sucks. Matter of fact, I wrecked my car that way. When they came out with, "Nobody can drink, not even you," I was like, "Oh fuck!" So, I drove home sober one day, and I wasn't concentrating like, you know, when you drink a lot, you pay attention. You're concentrating. I drove like shit sober. I mean, I worked like a whole night for a couple nights [after working days at a machine shop]. So, I hadn't had any sleep for like three days, and I was sober, and I'm driving home. So, I'm not concentrating like I do. There's a police cruiser sitting there, but I don't give a shit. I'm just driving home. But I fell asleep, man, right there! I hit a damn telephone pole. I called my wife, said, "I wrecked my car." "Where are you?" "I'm sitting in a cruiser with the cop." If I was drunk, I'd have been concentrating.

MIKE: That's valid.

JACK: Yeah, it is valid. Your bartender should be out there, in the game. We used to always drink a shot of Jameson at midnight [referring to himself and Laura, the other bartender who worked Fridays with Jack for several years]. That's what we did, and it was like, "Who else wants one?" We'd sell like six more shots that way, and we'd all toast. We made some money, everybody had a good time and we sold more Jameson. We don't sell a pittance of that now because we don't drink it. So, people don't see us drinking it and having a good time. I guess maybe we shouldn't be doing that kind of shit, but everybody had a good time doing it and we never went nuts.

MIKE: The world just isn't a fraction of as much fun as it used to be when I was younger, and I grew up in the "Just Say No" generation. The buzzkill was already well underway.

JACK: Yeah. Now, everybody's bitching about everything.

MIKE: A bartender shouldn't get drunk. I know from experience. You can't do the job competently if you are, but a bartender should have a few drinks.

JACK: Yeah. It's part of being conversational or relaxing. You might do a shot, you clean glasses and offer a little camaraderie. Arnold's is more corporate now. You get written up and shit.

MIKE: You got written up?!

JACK: Oh, yeah, called into the office and everything.

MIKE: What's a good, random story that expresses the vibe of Arnold's in the old days?

JACK: We used to have a telephone at Arnold's that sat on the back bar. So, when anybody got a call, it's like, "Here's the fucking telephone," and the line would go from the back bar across the bar. So, the line was strung across, and I'm in a big ass hurry, and I hit that line and pulled the whole telephone off the bar into the sink, into the soapy water. It's like a three-tier sink. When you wash glasses, you go soapy water, second sink, third sink. I just took that telephone, and I grabbed it out of the soapy water, dipped it in the second sink, then dipped in the third sink a couple of times, sat it down on the back bar. You know what? It quit working. But it was so spontaneous. It wasn't like, "Oh fuck!" I just picked it up out of the water and I dipped it.

I did it another time. There was a guy named Brownie. He had a set of false teeth. We were all bullshitting, and somebody said something so fucking funny that Brownie laughs out his teeth. They fell out of his mouth, bounced on the bar and fell into the soapy water. Again, without breaking a stride, I reached down and grabbed Brownie's teeth, dipped them a couple times in the second sink, dipped them in the third sink and snuck them back in his mouth. It was one of the funniest things ever. The spontaneous things were priceless. The telephone was pretty good, but at least Brownie's teeth worked again. The telephone didn't work. Then we got a wall phone. Those are my two sink stories. It's just not as fun now as it used to be.

MIKE: Do you think you'll ever quit?

JACK: Yeah, sometime. You gotta quit sometime. I'm going on sixty-three. The other day, I thought, "I want to be there 20 percent of Arnold's existence." I always thought that would be pretty cool. Then, the other day, I was thinking, "Oh shit, I went past that! I missed that one." Now, I'm thinking like 25 percent. When Arnold's is like 160, then I would have to be there forty years. So, it would be five more years. That's the new goal. I don't know. I don't feel like an old man.

MIKE: You've already been through a lot of momentous events. You were there when they introduced Christian Moerlein, one of the first craft beers in the country in '81, right?

JACK: Yeah, I tapped the first keg of it in our lifetime. Me and my wife were tending bar. They brought the beer in on a horse-drawn wagon, an old beer wagon. I brought it in, took it downstairs and tapped it. While they were trying to tap this ceremonial keg, I was already saying, "I tapped your first keg."

MIKE: You tapped the real one?

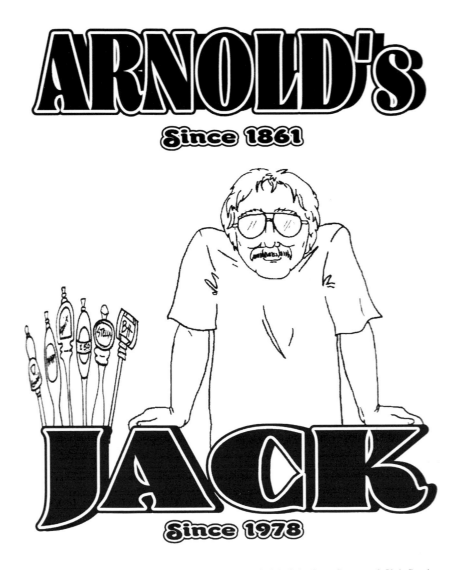

Arnold's celebrating Jack's fortieth-year anniversary behind the bar. *Courtesy of Chris Breeden, Arnold's Bar & Grill.*

JACK: Yeah, I did. While they were trying to tap the ceremonial one, me and my wife were at the bar drinking the beer. It was a really good beer. I actually tapped the first keg and drank the first beer before they tapped their "first keg." That was the staple at Arnold's for years and years.

MIKE: Yeah, I drank the hell out of five-dollar happy hour pitchers of it in '99.

JACK: I think we got Guinness before that. That was the first big beer thing there.

MIKE: Wasn't it the first Guinness in the city?

JACK: Us and Hap's Irish Pub got it on the same day. I'm going, "I don't like this," but people came from miles around—literally. We made so much money selling Guinness on tap because nobody else had it. We had it and Hap's. Then other people started getting it. We sold so much of it that it was super fresh.

Jack made it past his forty-year milestone. He could be found behind the bar at Arnold's until the start of COVID. He was, however, already battling cancer. He died in 2020, and the pandemic precluded the kind of remembrance of his life and his humor that he deserved. When this interview was recorded, it was hard to imagine Arnold's without Jack. Still is. Please take a moment to raise a drink in his honor, and make sure that it isn't some stupid fucking *Sex in the City* cocktail.

BOCKFEST

The Big Dirty Years

The ceremonial tapping release of Christian Moerlein Select at Arnold's Bar & Grill was an epic event seared into the public psyche, but when Francie Patton, who was responsible for special events at Hudepohl-Schoenling Brewing Company, was charged with planning the release of Moerlein's new bock beer in 1992, Arnold's wasn't her first choice. She wanted to plan an event in Mount Adams, the hippest, wettest, most popular nightlife destination in the city at the time. For all of Tarbell's force of personality, there still wasn't much going on downtown. Mount Adams, by contrast, already had too much drunken shenanigans for its civic leaders, so they told Ms. Patton and her dumb new beer to go pound salt. Kicked off the mountain, she went slumming, which brings us back to Tarbell.

Inspired by history—or at least a paraphrased version of it—Tarbell expanded the idea of a beer tapping to the resurrection of a nineteenth-century tradition, a city-wide celebration when all the city's German breweries tapped their spring bock beers at the same time. Historically speaking, this never happened. Most Cincinnati breweries did release a doppelbock in the spring, but they didn't do it on the same day or organize the release. Jim, however, never lets the truth get in the way of a good story. Enlisting the help of Over-the-Rhine advocates and organizers, like Julie Fay and several other early, influential rehabbers and bar owners, Francie, Jim and a nonprofit called Merchants of Main, formed largely to host the event, all started laying a vision for a first-year tapping and an annual festival. Paying homage to the city's ethnic history, it would be German themed, but it would focus on the Renaissance era rather than the nineteenth century. This was partially a literary, thematic nod to Over-the-Rhine's budding renaissance, but they also thought that the costumes would be more fun. There'd be monks and opulent royalty. *Bock* means "goat" in German, so, of course, there would be livestock. The pièce de résistance would be a parade that started at Arnold's, Cincinnati's oldest bar, traveled up Main Street into Over-the-Rhine, ending inside Old St. Mary's, Cincinnati's oldest church. Inside, the priest would bless the first ceremonial keg of the season's bock beer. Then the drinking of the bock would commence.

At the time, Over-the-Rhine was home to hundreds of vacant and condemned buildings, and it boasted the highest crime rate of any Cincinnati neighborhood. It had also become ground zero for a variety of homelessness and other social equity movements. As a result, the idea of Bockfest was bold, and it wasn't universally embraced. Beer Dave and the Oldenberg crew were there from the beginning, and he has a philosophical recollection on the scene.

DAVE: Early on, I remember thinking, "Wow, I've really made myself somebody in Cincinnati," because when we brought the kegs of beer to be blessed at Old St. Mary's, we were protested out front because, you know, beer was an evil thing to bring to Over-the-Rhine. Don't celebrate beer! They were out there with picket signs, and we were trying to get our keg of beer into the church and up to the altar to have it blessed.

Originally started by Hudepohl-Schoenling, Arnold's and the advocates that composed Merchants of Main, the festival was adopted by Barrel House Brewing Company, one of the city's great pioneer breweries in the 1990s. (There is a chapter dedicated to this brewery in *Cincinnati Beer*.) Barrel House shut down in 2005, and 2006 started a decade that some refer to as the "Mike Morgan era." Some of the challenges remained the same, some were different and some were self-

The spirit of Bockfest, an inclusive, multi-species celebration. *Courtesy of Alex Bell.*

made, usually with the help of too much beer. The neighborhood had passed through an early, nascent revival that collapsed after civil unrest in 2001, followed by a period of de-policing and resurgent crime. "OTR" wasn't the trendy place that it would become. Most of the bars that had thrived for a while in the late 1990s went out of business. It was gritty and dangerous, and so was its festival. Scott LaFollette captured the general feeling of those years.

❖ ❖ ❖

BRET: What was your first Bockfest like?

SCOTT: Oh, my God. My first Bockfest was back in the days when it was in closed-up bars on Main Street. That was the fucking Wild West! It really was fun.

BRET: Why was it so much fun?

111

SCOTT: Because Have a Nice Day Café, Rhythm & Blues Café, Jefferson Hall and these other places had been closed for like five years, and when they closed, they literally just turned the lights off and walked out. Five years later, you walked into those places, and it just smelled atrocious. It smelled like five-year-old vomit and mold.

MIKE: So, you started going when I ran it. I'd rent those closed bars for the weekend. Volunteers would come in and do a lot of work to make them useable for three days, get the toilets working, plug the coolers in, clean off the top layers of mold and grime, but they were like abandoned ghost bars.

SCOTT: Yeah, absolutely. It was when you were doing it and, yeah, absolutely fucking disgusting, but because of that, no one gave a shit about what happened. You weren't worried about spilling something on the floor, you weren't worried if your drunk buddy broke a table or whatever. And it was so underground. People were like, what the fuck is this? What's going on here? The year that it snowed, they were doing the homebrew competition, and I had to judge. The homebrew competition was in a place that had been a dance club. The place smelled like ass, and I'm trying to smell the beer, judge beer, over that smell of ass. Even the first few years when it was at the Christian Moerlein Brewery, the production place, those were pretty good too because it was still pretty underground. It was crazy, the wild things that really make memorable moments, the insane moments. You could probably do a whole book on just those early years of Bockfest. I know it was Bockfest long before that, the early '90s years, and the Barrel House years, but that's the period that I think of as the early years. It's weird how it became really popular and people forgot the roots.

MIKE: Immediately. I can assure you that almost everybody immediately forgot where everything started.

SCOTT: And it's like, why do you think this was popular in the first place? It's because it was fucking insane. It was grungy and weird, and you love illegal shit. You felt like you were in some kind of cool underground club of people. People who knew were like, "Yeah, dude, you know about Bockfest? We're going to go down there, but don't tell the squares."

MIKE: Yeah, I can tell you as the lawyer that ran it, we did a lot of illegal shit.

The former Jefferson Hall bar temporarily resurrected as Bockfest Hall. Yes, it was disgusting. *Courtesy of Alex Bell.*

SCOTT: Absolutely. It was pretty fucking sketchy. You'd be there and there were people having sex in a corner. It was like, I know this place can't be licensed to do this—whatever this is.

MIKE: In late 2005, I was hanging out at Arnold's. I was so much of a regular that I literally got mail there. I knew all the bartenders, like Jack, and Ronda Breeden, the owner, had become a friend. I asked Ronda when Bockfest 2006 was going to be because she was one of the organizers and because, back then, the date was always a moving target.

BRET: Isn't it always the first weekend in March?

MIKE: It is now, and you're welcome. I did that, and everybody hated me for it. Bockfest was related to Lent. Fat Tuesday is the last party before people give up gluttony for Lent, but Bockfest is the first party of Lent.

BRET: I didn't know that background.

MIKE: One of the legends about bock beer is that there were monks in Eisenbach, Germany, that thought it was a little drastic to give up drinking for Lent. Instead, they proposed to quit eating and just drink beer, a feat that has been attempted by multiple brewers in the city over the years. Which also explains why the style is so sweet. They made this beer that they loaded down with a bunch of malt, so it has more nutrients, calories, carbs, sugars. But once they had the beer, they had to get permission from the Vatican to drink during Lent. So, they sent a keg to Rome. It was a long trip, and the beer spoiled and soured on the way, so when it finally made it to the pope, it was terrible. The pope drank some of it, thought it was disgusting and therefore thought that it was a sufficient sacrifice for these monks to have to drink this terrible beer through Lent, so he blessed it. Thereafter, the monks of Eisenbach spent Lent getting hammered on this sweet, over-malted beer with a high ABV. That's why Bockfest is the opposite of Fat Tuesday. It's the celebration of just the first time that you'll be getting drunk on bock beer throughout Lent. Catholic or not, it's a fun concept, but the date was always different, and Covington used to have a big Mardi Gras festival that the Bockfest people didn't want to compete with, so there'd be arguments about the date of Bockfest a month before Bockfest. It was unworkable, and a couple of years into running it, I said, "It's the first weekend of March, this year and every year after 'til the end of time, and if you don't like that, screw you."

But I'm getting ahead of myself. Barrel House Brewing Company had been running it, organizing the parade, arranging the Bockfest Hall, getting the permits, doing the promotion, all the basic mechanics. Barrel House had gone out of business that year, and several of bars that used to participate had closed, so the consensus was that Bockfest probably wasn't going to happen. It was dead. Well, I had a pretty good buzz going, so I thought that was an unimaginable tragedy. I went into some deep, emotional lament like the reporter watching the Hindenburg go down in flames. I told Ronda that we had to save it—we had to run it if that was what was necessary. She said, "OK, I'll bring the bars together and we can have meetings here, if you'll organize the parade, get all the permits and do all that stuff. You're willing to do that?" "Absolutely!" I agreed because I was kind of drunk. The next day, I sobered up and I realized what I'd committed to. I didn't know the first fucking thing about running a parade or a festival, getting street permits or liquor permits, doing press releases and promotion. I'd never done anything like that. The people who were around that still had a role in the festival were all highly opinionated and disagreed with each other and me on basically everything. So, rather than getting any help, I had a half dozen people constantly bitching at me. There was a zero-dollar budget, and due to some past events, the Cincinnati Police hated the parade. It was a terrible idea for me to agree to do it, but I knew a guy back then who said that the test of a real man is whether he does sober the things that he commits to when he's drunk. I thought, yeah, I'm a real man, baby. So I guess I'm running a festival. That's how it all got started. I agreed to do something stupid when I was drunk.

BRET: What was the first Bockfest that you ran like?

MIKE: A bit of a cluster and anemic. Bockfest had grown in the '90s, then started to thin out after 2001, so the crowds were sparse, and I had my hands full just trying to make basic things happen, like get a parade down the street without getting arrested, getting posters printed, sending a press release. I managed to get $500 in sponsorship from Huff Realty. That was the entire budget. It was probably the worst Bockfest in history, but I pulled it off. It was going to die, and I kept it alive. It also got into my blood. I wanted to do it again, and I wanted to keep making it bigger and better.

BRET: What was the first step?

MIKE: The first thing was to extend the hours and to bring the hall back. It was only something that happened on Friday night at that point. In all previous years, there had been a Bockfest Hall in a temporary space that was open on Friday and usually Saturday too. In the early days, it was a way to show off the potential of vacant space in the neighborhood. So, I extended it to Saturday in 2007, rented a vacant space to use as a hall. I got volunteers from the nonprofit Brewery District CURC to clean it—sort of—and I got more sponsorship support. I'd started to understand promotion, so it got good media coverage too, and it grew.

BRET: Is that when it started to really blow up?

MIKE: Nope. That's when the wheels came off. The next year is what is remembered as Snow Bockalypse. This year was going to be the breakaway year. I rented a big space that used to be a nightclub called the Red Cheetah. Huge! I ordered a gazillion kegs. Saturday was better planned, with historic brewery tours. We got great press coverage. I sort of knew what I was doing, and it was teed up to be a lot bigger than it had ever been. On the day of the parade, it started to snow—a lot. I started getting calls from the city manager's office saying, "We might have some problems here." I had a good relationship with the city manager at the time, and he supported me and Bockfest both, so he was trying to help, but eventually he called to say that Hamilton County was declaring a stage-whatever snow emergency. It was the biggest blizzard in thirty or forty years, and it all came down the day of the parade, in a matter of hours. It was illegal for anybody to drive anywhere except the hospital. Obviously, that meant that they pulled my parade permit.

But a lot of people congregated at Arnold's anyway, where the parade was supposed to start. Tarbell was there with a lot of the regulars from the parade, including the guys who always pulled the big Trojan Goat in monks' robes, which is still the most iconic part of the parade. The goat was out front. Arnold's motorized bathtub was gassed up. Everybody decided that we we're going to have a parade anyway. Tarbell was vice-mayor, and he invoked some powers that didn't really exist. The vice-mayor of Cincinnati walks out of the bar with a beer, in a court jester costume, followed by all the monks and a bunch of people already half-drunk on doppelbock, and he announces some bullshit emergency declaration requiring that the show must go on. And in violation of a bunch of actual, legally enforceable emergency orders, an illegal Bockfest Parade started moving up Main Street in a blizzard. It was the complete collapse of months of incredible work and planning, but it was beautiful in a way. A lot of people remember it as their favorite parade. The few people that could walk there had fun, but financially it was a disaster.

BRET: I bet it was. How does Bockfest even recover from something like that? What happens the next year? Were people philosophical about it?

MIKE: Hell no! I moved Bockfest around with me, and I ran it through the nonprofit that I was working for in 2008. I brought it. It was my festival, and I did most of the work, but they wanted to cancel it because they thought that year proved that it was a waste of time and it couldn't make money. I worked for the board, but I just ignored them and started planning 2009. Later, when I grew it to the point that it started making money, those motherfuckers claimed that they owned it. There was a lot of that. Small thinking when I was growing it, then getting in line to steal my work product when it started to succeed.

I thought that we needed to have a ceremony to control the weather, to prevent another blizzard. I wanted to sacrifice something, but I didn't want to kill anything. Steve Hampton, who also became a primary organizer, said, "Why don't we burn a snowman?" He's a smart guy, so I was dumbfounded. "I'm not a chemist, but I'm pretty sure that it's going to be really fucking hard to get snow to burn, Steve." He clarified that we'd make one out of papier-mâché or something, burn it in effigy. It was a brilliant idea, so Precipitation Retaliation was born. One week before the parade, I gave some ridiculous speech, tried the snowman for crimes against Bockfest in Old West lynch mob style, and we'd set it on fire.

BRET: Did it work?

MIKE: It never snowed again, and 2009 was a great success. But I had to start making a lot of functional changes that pissed people off. I spent a lot of time and energy arguing with what felt like everybody in the neighborhood. A lot of people called me the "Mayor of Over-the-Rhine" back then, but my chosen title was "Bockfest Czar." Everything was run by committee, and I showed up to a meeting one day and just declared myself in charge, declared myself a dictator. I didn't have any real, objective authority. It caused some people to hate me, but it was the right thing to do and several of those people became close friends.

The first major thing I changed was the date, making it the first weekend in March by dictatorial decree. Everybody said that I would kill the festival the first time that it wound up being the same weekend as Covington Mardi Gras. Instead, by the time that happened, Bockfest had grown so much that Covington changed its date because they couldn't compete with Bockfest.

I also extended it to become a solid two-day event with some limited stuff happening on Sunday. Later, Sunday was expanded too. But it was really challenging to talk people into just making it even a two-day event. When I started running it, Mr. Pitiful's was one of the Main Street bars that had survived the die-off. It's on the parade route, and the whole front of the bar is a bunch of windows, which makes it one of the best places to watch the parade. But it wasn't until year four of me as Bockfest Czar that Pitiful's agreed to open early for the parade. By "early" I mean 5:30 or 6:00, when they typically opened at seven or eight. They repeatedly told me that they weren't going to do enough business from the Bockfest Parade to justify paying for the electric for an extra hour, hour and a half.

BRET: All twenty-five cents of that electric bill.

MIKE: Exactly. In their defense, 2006 sucked and there was a blizzard in 2008, but they just couldn't see what I could. Once they got it, those guys loved me. I could almost never pay for a drink there. Eventually, that was true of all the Main Street bars. I made a lot of people a lot of money. Unfortunately, I wasn't one of them, but I did drink for free in Over-the-Rhine for about ten years. They all had to be brought around, though. I had to beg and browbeat them to open on Saturday afternoons, and it was always same conversation. "Nobody is ever going to come to Bockfest on a Saturday." Then, when they'd open for the first time and business was slow, they'd bitch at me, but I sold the vision hard enough that they hung in. The next year got better, then the one after that, and by the time I was done running the festival, Bockfest Saturday had become the single most profitable day of the year for several of those bars, and Friday was the second.

Ronda Breeden, former owner of Arnold's Bar & Grill and the woman who talked Mike into running Bockfest, awards the winning parade entry with this year's trophy, a scale model of Old St. Mary's Church, made by artist J.K. Smith, standing behind and to her left. (Don Heinrich Tolzmann, author and German American historian, is behind and to her right.) *Courtesy of Alex Bell.*

BRET: Why did it grow? What was the key to it?

MIKE: It was several primary things. First, I focused a lot on growing the parade. I didn't know anything about running parades. I also hated parades. When I thought of parades, I thought about fire engines, politicians, high school marching bands—all that boring nonsense. Then, I was in New Orleans. At the time, only one of the Mardi Gras parades went through the French Quarter, and it was a week before the bigger parades that most people think of as Mardi Gras weekend. It's called Krewe du Vieux, and it had a reputation for being the edgiest of the parades, very political, irreverent, semi-profane with a lot of sexual themes. We weren't there to see it intentionally. I didn't know it existed. I just happen to be in the Quarter drinking a beer on a street corner, and this huge float with a big set of breasts on the front of it like an eighteenth-century ship—if it were owned by Larry Flynt—just comes rolling up the street like a fever dream, trailing all these great bands, more crazy floats and a sea of drunk people. Instead of candy, people on the floats are tossing condoms. It changed everything. I'm like, "Goddamn, that's what I want!" That's the parade I want for Bockfest, the Cincinnati version!

Once I had the inspiration, I had to figure out how to get people to do it. I started with a trophy. I knew that I had to incentivize people to put effort into building interesting floats. A big cash prize would have been great, but we still didn't have any money. If the incentive couldn't be objectively valuable, it needed to be cool, something motivational. The glass campus of the Art Academy was in the neighborhood then, and they agreed to do a huge, hand-blown glass trophy. We had a little event around it that we called the Bockfest Blow. Ronda from Arnold's catered it. We brought beer. It became an annual thing, and the trophies kept getting bigger and cooler. I went around with sketches of the trophy, fliers, putting them up in bars, asking clubs to build floats, asking the participating bars to build floats. Dan Listermann would come down and literally brew a batch of beer on a flatbed truck as they rolled down the street tossing hops at people. Groups of friends and neighbors in Over-the-Rhine formed float krewes. Originally, I was running around begging people to build something for it, but it started to grow organically, kept getting bigger and weirder, exactly what I wanted. At some point, the Art Academy people stopped making the trophy for a while, but I found other artists. My friend J.K. Smith was an amazing wood artist and made some incredible pieces, so we still had these great works of art that groups competed with each other to win. That helped grow both the parade and the weirdness.

BRET: Cool, but you're not saying that a trophy turned the whole thing around, are you?

MIKE: No. It was multiple fronts, tons of work. Getting news coverage was easier back then. In those days, I put a lot of time into building personal relationships with entertainment reporters and TV news producers. That mattered back then. You didn't need to do YouTube stories and constant posts on Facebook, Twitter, Instagram, TikTok. It was still a lot of work, but one person could handle all the media promotion for it if you built the relationships and you kept giving people some new angle every year, some new little bit of weirdness.

BRET: Like Sausage Queen.

MIKE: Exactly. By the second year I did it, I had become the director of a nonprofit called the Over-the-Rhine Foundation. The previous, retiring director was a woman named Marge Hammelrath. She'd done a lot of great things for the neighborhood, and she'd been part of Bockfest from the beginning. Like several people, she had a role that she played every year. Marge would walk in the parade in a German medieval costume carrying a tray of sausages, and they called her the "Sausage Queen." I obviously saw the innuendo, and I didn't intend to personally become the new Sausage Queen. In 2007, we had a very tame, family-friendly, tongue-in-cheek competition at Arnold's to crown that year's queen. There were only two contestants. One was a woman in a Renaissance-era princess costume. The other was a guy that was a bit tipsy and decided that he was going to compete. He was in one of the beer bands, dressed in lederhosen, funny guy. It was beauty pageant styled, but they were going to be judged mostly on talent, and I wrote the rules to define that as "whatever talent you think a Sausage Queen should have." They were both entertaining, and we made them both queen. Not king and queen, but co-queens, and the gender-neutral aspect of the competition took off.

Later that year, I went to the Mardi Gras Museum in Mobile, Alabama, which is where Mardi Gras actually started, not in New Orleans. I wound up basing several aspects of Bockfest on modified Mardi Gras traditions. First, Mardi Gras is not just a weekend or Fat Tuesday, it's a month or more of events and traditions that lead up to Mardi Gras parades. A lot of old-school fraternal organizations and groups of different interests and compositions have balls during Mardi Gras, and they nominate or elect their kings and queens, who then represent them in the parades. It's prestigious, a serious honor. So, I decided to bastardize the concept, make it a raucous, innuendo-laden thing that would take place in neighborhood bars and dives across the city during the "Bockfest Season." Each location would have its competition, like a Mardi Gras ball, but rude and crude and funny, and each bar would vote for its Sausage Queen Princess. All the princesses would be in the parade, and then one of them would win the final competition at Bockfest. Some of the hardest times I've laughed in my entire life were during the first few years of Sausage Queen competitions. Obviously, you had to have a good sense of humor and not take yourself too seriously to do it, and so many of these contestants did the most hilarious, unexpected things. The competitions were also meant to be guerrilla marketing, a way to get people from different parts of the city to buy into Bockfest, hopefully build a float for their princess, then show up at the competition. Like Mardi Gras, it also turned Bockfest into more of a full season of events and traditions, including the Bockfest Blow, Precipitation Retaliation, pre-festival tappings. I started wishing people "Happy Bockfest" starting in the first week of February.

David Morgan, a multiple-year Sausage Queen contestant and member of the secretive Royal International Sausage Queen Commission, which was previously in charge of "organizing" and conducting the competition, poses with a Sausage Queen contestant. (Amy and Mike Morgan are drunk in the background.) *Courtesy of Alex Bell.*

BRET: At some point, Moerlein became a big part of it. What was the relationship there?

MIKE: After I'd started running it, I think it was 2007, Greg Hardman got my number from somebody and called me. He had recently bought Christian Moerlein and the brands that came with it. I'd never met him. He called me and said, "I really want to be a part of Bockfest. I like what you're doing, and I want to support it. I want my beers to be part of it." I'm like, great, because I was trying to find beer sponsors, and nobody would give me the time of day. The breweries either didn't have any money or just wouldn't give me any, or they'd want to become a major sponsor for $200. Greg didn't write a fat check either, but he brought a lot of direct help with infrastructure, promotion, marketing. He had a lot of festival experience and he had staff, and I was kicking ass for not knowing what I was doing but I was flying blind. So, Moerlein really helped it grow. When it got bigger, there were also more breweries popping up, and they started wanting to be part of it. That was great, and I wanted to have a lot of breweries involved. I wanted it to be a city-wide celebration, but I was also very loyal to Hardman and Moerlein. He understood what I was trying to build back when rich distributors wouldn't return my calls and bar owners were busting my balls over the cost of electric.

As an attorney, I also acquired the production facility for the Christian Moerlein Brewing Company that they had in Over-the-Rhine. That produced a couple of my favorite Bockfest moments. After over a year of irritating negotiations with some scumbag in Texas, I got part of the former Kauffman Brewery under contract. It had a great history. It had also been the Hussman Potato Chip factory. So, it was grandfathered as a food production facility, but it also had this gorgeous nineteenth-century malt room with lagering cellars under it. I still think that it remains the most perfectly suited brewery building in the city, but we're talking about north of Liberty Street in 2009–10, adjacent to a park that had more murders than any other address in the city. It was the Wild West, so I also had to get private financing for part of it to make the deal go through, and everything about the transaction continued to be a pain in the ass through closing. Once the contract and the financing were finalized, I decided to move Bockfest Hall to that building and to keep it there. By 2009, south Over-the-Rhine was in the ascent again. There were still vacant spaces, but nobody wanted to rent me a huge bar for a weekend if it might hinder their ability to lease it to a real tenant.

BRET: A space that's going to have drunken shenanigans happening in it, no less.

MIKE: Yeah, that too. In 2009, I didn't have a hall secured until two weeks before the festival. I had to have an embarrassing conversation with an entertainment reporter that I knew well by then. She said, "It's really hard for me to help you promote this festival if you don't even know where it's going to be." Yeah, that's fair. The places we rented were also always shitholes, and it took an army of volunteers days of work just to get them functionally filthy. It was a fun idea, but it was no longer workable. I needed a place that could consistently serve as the hall, and we were finally supposed to close on the new Moerlein brewery building the week of Bockfest 2010. I had the liquor license for that location, had the address in all the advertisements. That building was Bockfest Hall, but there was a problem with the money transfer, so we couldn't close the deal on time. It was going to close, but not until the Monday after Bockfest. The ownership structure was complicated, and I had gotten access to the space. Under the assumption that everything was going to transfer by the time a parade and several thousand people ended up inside the building at about 7:00 that night, we'd set everything up, but it was still going to effectively be owned by some scumbag debt collection firm in Texas. Everybody started freaking out, asking me what I was going to do, telling me that I obviously couldn't hold a festival in a building that we didn't have the legal right to occupy, but what was I going to do? Call it off? I said, "I'm going to have a Bockfest. They're in Texas. Fuck them. I've got the key, a liquor license and a massive amount of beer. Full steam ahead." That's what we did. It was still an underground kind of thing, but it was getting pretty big by then. There were thousands of people through that building over the course of that weekend, dozens and dozens of kegs drained, stages set up, bands, Sausage Queen competition, homebrew competition and a whole parade coming right into the building—and everybody was trespassing. That was the spirit of Bockfest back when it was fun.

BRET: Yeah, but things change eventually.

MIKE: They do, but let me tell you my other favorite Bockfest moment. It was part of the same series of events. Originally, the parade route ended in Old St. Mary's Church, but Bockfest got kicked out of the church long before me, and the parade was ending at an arbitrary place in the street. There were always problems with that too, and it didn't make any sense.

The Bockfest Parade starts to form outside Arnold's Bar & Grill. *Courtesy of Michael D. Morgan.*

So, that year I changed the route of the parade to go across Liberty, west on McMicken and end in the new Bockfest Hall. There was exactly one person in the city of Cincinnati that thought that was a good idea, and that was me. Universally 100 percent of everybody else thought I was making a massive mistake. Several people told me that there was no doubt that somebody was going to get shot, and I'd be responsible. I said, "Probably not. We won't know until we do, but I can tell you that we're gonna do it." I used to drive my Cadillac convertible in the parade, and the most heartwarming moment of my time with Bockfest—my single favorite moment—was when I rolled across Liberty, turned on McMicken and the street was lined with people out in front of their houses on McMicken, kids waving, guys grilling—no urban apocalypse, just everybody having a great time. It was beautiful. That became the parade route after that, and nobody said another word about it—including not telling me that I was right, of course.

BRET: So, you're building momentum. You've got this kind of cool, underground thing, but all cool things grow to a point where they're not as cool anymore. When did it start to go off the rails?

MIKE: I can tell you precisely. 2012 was the year. That was the pinnacle of the Sausage Queen competition. Originally, you had to talk people into doing it. You go on stage and do something silly so that you can be called the "Sausage Queen." But I had gotten enough publicity with that competition that it became blood sport that year. Contestants took it really seriously, putting a lot of work into their acts and their costumes. We used to judge it in purely arbitrary ways, wearing buttons that said that we took bribes. It was a blast, but I didn't want to judge it anymore because people were getting pissed off because they didn't win. And everybody that entered that year was really good, and the crowd for it was amazing—people packed into this huge hall to watch this stupid little thing that I'd started in a couple of dive bars. It was the best one ever, but it had run its full course.

I'd started hiring buses that stopped at the bars and circulated people through the neighborhood, and the buses stopped at the Garfield Suites as our official hotel. They were a sponsor, and I used to get a penthouse for free to use as Bockfest command headquarters. I did use it as a quiet place to deal with problems, talk to the press and whatever, but I mostly used it to decompress or get high. So, I'm standing on this huge balcony with some random people, talking to two women from Nashville who had heard about Bockfest and had come up to check it out. They'd been enjoying it, and one of them said to me, "You know, this is your perfect moment. You still have to kind of be in-the-know to know that this thing exists, but at the same time, it's big. It's big enough to be a thing, but it's still underground enough that it's cool. It can't stay that way, you know. Nothing can. It's going to lose that." She wasn't being mean, and I'm grateful that she let me see it in time to appreciate it, but it was like a gut punch. I knew she was right, and she was. After that year, the greed really started to take hold with people, started to strangle the cool and the fun out of it.

BRET: From an outsider's perspective, it's still just as big as ever.

MIKE: Oh, it's gotten much bigger and people love it, but people love Oktoberfest and Taste of Cincinnati and other events that I think are completely soulless and that I don't understand. The more soulless an event is, the more welcoming it is to the masses.

BRET: There's something thrilling about the taste of real freedom, skirting the law, doing things that are socially taboo to a wider audience. That kind of cool doesn't last forever.

MIKE: It doesn't. Those years were gritty. We crossed a lot of lines. In the end, once it started to get profitable, I was forced out of my own festival. But my friend Ronda Breeden from Arnold's, who talked me into getting involved in the first place, used to tell me, "We keep doing this because for one weekend out of the year, we're rock stars in this city." It was an exaggeration, but it felt that way. It was fun as hell while it lasted.

LINDSEY MARIE BONADONNA

Rise of Goose Island and Collapse of Rivertown

Rivertown Brewing Company was opened in 2009 by partners Randy Shiltz and Jason Roeper. It was an early pioneer in the local craft beer renaissance of the 2000s, opened at a time when production and distribution were the required business model. Taproom sales weren't a thing yet. It was pre–Blank Slate, pre–Mad Tree, pre-Rhinegeist. Their goal for the first year was 500 barrels, but the beer was good, the market was hot and their timing was right, so they sold 1,500 barrels instead. Rivertown grew rapidly, but the two founding partners had some differences of vision and decided to go their separate ways. Along the way, Jason married Lindsey Marie Bonadonna, a woman with her own intriguing history with the burgeoning craft beer revolution. After Randy left Rivertown to open Wooden Cask Brewing Company in Newport, Kentucky, Lindsey started playing an increasingly crucial role in Rivertown. Unfortunately, Rivertown didn't have a fairytale ending on either the domestic or business fronts. Lindsey and Jason got divorced, and directly unrelated, Rivertown found itself in a precarious financial position and permanently closed its doors in 2022. We talked to Lindsey about her early days in beer, her role at Rivertown and life afterward.

◆ ◆ ◆

MIKE: Your introduction to the craft beer business started well before Rivertown.

LINDSEY: I got involved in the beer industry in 2005. I'm originally from Buffalo, New York, and moved—kind of randomly—to Findlay, Ohio, where I had some friends. I was bartending and doing bookkeeping for my friend's bar, and that is where I was first introduced to craft beer. Honestly, I grabbed a Goose Island's Kilgubbin Irish Red Ale because I liked the label. From there, my next craft beer was a Sierra Nevada Celebration Ale. Again, I liked the label. But when I was working at the bar, I developed great relationships with different distributors, and I was approached about taking a position as a craft and import specialty rep at the local Anheuser-Busch division. This was sometime in the early 2000s. At that time, A.B.'s craft portfolio looked like Red Hook and Widmer, and that was it. Imports were Hoegaarden, Leffe and Stella Artois. The distributor was very small, and that team really instilled my love of craft. They sent me different places. I started doing beer dinners. This is way back in the day, so people thought it was super cool.

MIKE: Yeah, I remember those days. I used to do beer dinners with Christian Moerlein. People went crazy over them.

LINDSEY: During that time, Goose Island would pop up at lot, and I would always go to my boss and say, "Man, I wish we could distribute Goose Island. When can we distribute Goose Island?" But those relationships are complicated; they couldn't just switch distributors. So, a couple years into working for Beerco [a distributorship in Findlay, Ohio], my boss called me and told me to come back into the office. He's very serious. He also liked to mess with me quite a bit, but he's like, "You need to come back. We have something to tell you." I'm freaking out on a forty-minute drive from the boonies back to Beerco.

MIKE: You're driving for forty minutes wondering if it's good news or you're about to get fired?

LINDSEY: Yes! So, I got back, and they sat me down in front of a TV to watch the announcement that we were going to start distributing Goose Island. And I just about lost it. They sent me to Chicago. I got to go work with the brewers at Goose Island. It was such a cool experience.

BRET: So, you were there for what people call the original selling out of craft?

LINDSEY: I was, yeah. I built my relationship with Goose Island selling it as a local rep for the distributorship, and I was eventually presented with an opportunity to become a sales rep exclusively for Goose Island. So, I was with Goose through the buyout, which was a really interesting experience to go through, and I think I have a different perspective than most people do on it. I covered Ohio, Kentucky, Indiana and Michigan, which today seems like an insane amount of territory for a brewery.

BRET: What is your perspective on it?

LINDSEY: We weren't often called out to Chicago, so it was weird that we had the whole team called out, all hands on deck. We thought that we were going to be told that we had been acquired by the Craft Brewers Alliance. We already had a relationship with them. Strategically, it would have made sense. So, we were all hanging out speculating about that on the morning of the announcement. We were all gathered in the loading dock at the brewery, a hundred or so of us, all standing around waiting for John Hall's announcement [the founder of Goose Island Brewing]. And I don't know who did it, but someone posted from Goose Island's social media account that we were bought by Anheuser-Busch. So, the word spread very quickly amongst us before John's official announcement to us, and it was not received well. But here's my take. It was always John's dream to be a national brewery, and the fact was that Goose Island was landlocked. There was no way to expand the brewery. As we know, making beer does not make you rich. It's a labor of love. The money wasn't there to build a new brewery, and I think John was presented with an opportunity to get his dream, and he went after it. And I think that's something that a lot of people don't appreciate.

Then there were different periods in time where the sales team was brought in to do triangle taste testing, especially when we had to expand production to meet the needs of the AB's Baldwinsville Brewery [an Anheuser-Busch branch in New York]. And I can tell you that the IPA brewed in Baldwinsville was significantly better than the version brewed in Chicago. Regardless of how we all feel about big breweries—and I have a complicated relationship with them—they know how to make consistent product. Being in business, you sometimes have to make hard decisions. I can understand from the business side why John made the decision he made. From the heart side, I think it was tough.

I ended up leaving Goose Island because I was presented with a six-figure salary, big title high-end regional manager position in Chicago. I decided not to take it because I was like, one day I'm gonna have to either sell something I don't feel passionate about or I'm gonna have to do a ton of spreadsheets, and I don't want that.

BRET: So, you quit because they offered you too much money and status?

LINDSEY: Yeah, that was my thought process. I was probably around twenty-nine or thirty then. We had started Cincinnati Beer Week. I was one of the founders, and we were working through all of that around the time I left Goose Island, and it's also when I met Jason, and we started dating. At that time, Rivertown had been open for over a year. They were one of the few local breweries in the area around 2010, 2011.

I worked at Apple for a while. It was a super transformative experience, changed my life in a lot of ways, but I was only there for six months. Then, I got sucked back into beer, back into the wholesale side.

MIKE: You left Goose Island and got out of the industry completely, and you were doing something that you really enjoyed. Was it Rivertown that sucked you back into beer?

LINDSEY: No. I was approached by Heidelberg Distributing. They wanted to talk to me about a position that they were creating, essentially the craft sales manager over their Dayton and Cincinnati Anheuser-Busch branches. As much as I enjoyed working at Apple, when you love something, you love something. It felt like a dream job at the time. I was in charge of educating the sales team. I got to do beer dinners and all of that.

MIKE: I was doing beer dinners back then too, around 2007, 2008. They were a big thing. We'd always sell them out, and it would blow people's minds when they'd get really good pairings that they didn't expect, like a really nice, clean pilsner with a salad or a dessert with the right porter. They can still be great events, but they had their day, then they were all over the place, then everybody quit giving a shit. Like ceremonial tappings and festivals. Oversaturation.

LINDSEY: Yeah, I really love doing beer and wine throwdowns, to give people a context of how these two things interact differently with food. I'm just remembering how many times I was challenged on my knowledge, which was exhausting sometimes, but I also felt proud, because it's like, "Yeah, I actually know what I'm talking about—surprise!"

MIKE: Do you think that gender was a significant part of being questioned on your knowledge, or was that just incidental?

LINDSEY: I feel like I look a little bit differently at the women in beer thing because back then there was me and like a handful of other women, but not many. I may have been the only one in the immediate area in the business, and I do think that it caused some people to want to boost their egos, or show off their knowledge or make me feel small by asking me the craziest questions that nobody in a million years even gives a shit about, even like the nerdiest homebrewer.

BRET: Homebrewers love to try to stump people like that. It's crazy.

LINDSEY: Yeah, it's an ego thing. I can see that very clearly now, but in the moment, I just kind of used it to make sure that I knew what I was talking about. But I'm also humble enough say, "You know what? I actually don't know the answer to that, but let's find out together." Kill them with kindness. But yeah, I don't think I would have been questioned the same way if I was a dude.

BRET: Very nice way to put that.

LINDSEY: Yeah, I'm trying to keep it nice. There was also some misunderstood humor.

MIKE: You've got to elaborate on that one.

LINDSEY: I'll keep this story short, but I think it's very funny. When I was with Goose Island and I covered all of Ohio, there was one time that I was at a distributor in Lancaster, Ohio. We had a very early morning sales meeting where they wanted me to do beer education, so I brought all these beers. I'm in a room full of what I'd call "traditional large brewery sales reps." You know, polo shirts, mustaches, lots of golfing. When I do beer education, I like to try to narrow it down to two words to represent a style. That way, if you can just remember one or two words, you can generally talk about the style. So, we get up to Honkers IPA. I say, "The two words that I like to use to describe IPA are dry and bitter—you know, like your old lady." I'm thinking that was the funniest thing in the world, but it was just crickets. They're all just staring at me. I was like, "Come on. That was funny!" But later I found out that it's cool if dudes talk to each other about their old ladies, but it's not as cool when a woman talks about somebody's old lady.

BRET: It's too real when you do it. It's like, I'm just drinking beer here. Now you're reminding me of what's going on at home.

MIKE: You were working at Heidelberg, and you were dating Jason Roeper, who was running Rivertown with Randy Shiltz. You loved your job, and they were doing really well, so how did you make the move to Rivertown?

LINDSEY: I got pregnant.

MIKE: That's exactly how Bret went from Cargill to Urban Artifact. He got pregnant.

Lindsey Marie Bonadonna and her daughter, Presley, in the Rivertown taproom. *Courtesy of Lindsey Marie Bonadonna.*

LINDSEY: I find out that I'm expecting while I'm with Heidelberg, and I work there the whole time that I'm pregnant, which I think adds a fun layer to the beer industry. After I had our daughter, Presley, I had every intention of going back to Heidelberg because I loved the work that I was doing there, but time drug on, and I wound up staying home with Presley for a couple years. I was also dabbling in the brewery stuff, keeping my hands in what was going on. Around that time, Jason and Randy decided to part ways. That's another story that I feel like a lot of people dramatized, but they just had two different visions for the business. I think what we see with Randy at the Wooden Cask is Randy's vision of what he had wanted for Rivertown, and I really enjoy going there because those beers are solid! He brews more traditional beers, and I miss some of those traditional styles at times. During the time when they were splitting ways, I started getting involved more in small ways—nothing huge, a lot of marketing, asking how we wanted people to feel about the brand, what do the labels look like? How is the team doing? I was involved, but not full-time involved. Then, we needed to expand. We were doing a lot of contract work for Kroger and Trader Joe's, and we were brewing on a thirty-barrel system in Lockland. Similar to Goose Island's problem. Jason decided to expand Rivertown and started looking at different properties, and I was kind of like, "Hell yeah! Go for it! I believe in what you're doing. I believe in the liquid. I love that we're doing more sours." I was along for the ride.

MIKE: Was a big part of the split between Jason and Randy a fundamental disagreement about the kind of styles they should be brewing?

LINDSEY: I never got that impression. I think it was a combination of how big the brewery should get and also the balance of styles. I wasn't with them 24/7, but I never picked up on a tension like Jason was saying, "We're only doing sours," and Randy was saying, "We're only doing traditional styles." I think they just had two divergent thought paths, and it was predominantly a difference of opinion on growth. Jason wanted more rapid growth. Randy also wanted growth, of course, but I think Randy was more comfortable slowing down and enjoying it because there's so much that can happen with growth. In my current business venture, I'm cool with taking it slow and letting things unfold rather than setting some arbitrary number at some point in time.

BRET: I was just having that conversation with the owner of Narrow Path Brewing Company when you walked up. At what point can you just get off the treadmill and decide that enough is enough? Can you just chill at a set volume and be happy with how much you're making? Do you have to constantly grow like a tumor? What is the point? Can you feel it when you're there? I don't think I'm there yet, but I want that feeling.

LINDSEY: Well, that's the blessing and the curse of being an entrepreneur. We have been blessed with drive. Even when we want to slow down and just enjoy what is going on and be present in the moment, there's still always something that comes up, or there's an opportunity.

Jason looked at quite a few places, and he decided Monroe was best because of its location, seeing how Cincinnati and Dayton were growing closer to each other. And the City of Monroe was very supportive. I think successful breweries today are going to be in neighborhoods where there's lots of foot traffic. Even though the concept of the Monroe location was great, it was not easily accessible—not walkable to anything.

BRET: No, it was 100 percent a destination. Whether it's intentional or not, it seems like you have a very good eye for getting involved in the thick of things right as transition is occurring. I don't know whether you're drawn to transitory change or you cause it, but it's a recurring theme.

LINDSEY: That's wild. I never thought about it that way. When you're in the thick of things, you don't actually realize how much you're doing or what you're taking on. Then, when you're removed and you reflect back, you're like, how the fuck did we get all that done?

MIKE: I understand the need for Rivertown's expansion, but what is a mystery to us is all the change that you took on at once. It was a twenty-six-thousand-square-foot facility with four-thousand square feet of restaurant space, $6 million of expansion, also coupled with changing damn near everything else about the business. You got rid of the Roebling Vanilla Porter, which had been revolutionary in this area and put Rivertown on the map; focused on sours and funkier styles; and changed all the branding. And it's not like the formula was broken. For the first few years, Rivertown grew 100 percent every year. It was doing fantastic, so what was the rationale behind shaking everything up at the same time?

LINDSEY: Yeah. I could see why people would ask, "What is Rivertown doing with all the sours?" In fact, there were just two in the regular lineup and an expansion of the barrel aging program. But for me, it was just a freshening of what it looked like, because I love marketing and image. It was like, we have this new building and a new restaurant, so we need some new branding. To me, being in the thick of it, it all just made sense that we would do all of this at one time and have a rebirth. But yeah, as you reflect it back to me, I can see where that would be like, "WTF is going on over here?"

BRET: You were ahead of the curve pushing even two sour brands as mainstays in 2014–15. Everyone likes to joke that Cincinnati is behind the times, but it often is, and that shows with sour beers. Sours have existed for centuries, and just in craft beer they've been around for a lot longer than 2015, but they blew people's brains here then. People thought it was crazy.

LINDSEY: There are biological reason why beers like sours and IPAs are challenging for us. In my field testing, I've gotten enough data to support this. If you look at a typical person's beer journey, they always start with something malty, or often with wheat beers; then they can get to an IPA. In some sensory panel I did, I think with Goose Island, they talked about the importance of tasting things three times before you make a decision because the first time it's your caveman brain telling you that drinking something bitter is poisonous, it's going to kill you, so that's the first reaction. The second reaction of our brain is, "Hmm, you took another sip even though I warned you, and I see that we're not dying." Then, by the third sip, that part of our brain—the amygdala—has calmed down enough to be like, "Okay, do we like this or not?" Sours are the next step after IPAs because our response to sours is, "This is spoiled, we're going to get really sick from this."

MIKE: Bret and I have also observed that the consumer needs to relate to a flavor that they're already familiar with. Then you can take them almost anywhere. You can even do something batshit crazy like a pickle beer because it still tastes like something that the consumer can understand. Conversely, you can brew something absolutely brilliant, like the Phrenology that Bret used to do, which was an IPA made with *Brettanomyces*. It was a complex combination of a bunch of hops and a really funky yeast, nuanced, delicious, like nothing else, and it didn't sell because people couldn't relate it to anything else they'd ever tasted. But he can sell the shit out of pickle beer because people know what pickles taste like. So, there's also that mental block too.

Cincinnati women in the beer industry team up to brew a special collaborative beer for International Women's Day. Lindsey is in the back row, far right. Roxanne Westendorf, who runs the Missing Ingredient Homebrew Competition for Missing Linck Fest, is front row, center. *Courtesy of Lindsey Marie Bonadonna.*

What you're saying about evolutionary instincts feels spot-on, and I think those things feed each other. We're very accustomed to sugar, for example, so people can't seem to buy enough awful, sickly sweet pastry stouts.

LINDSEY: Yeah, they're disgusting but they're sugar, and we're addicted to that as a culture right now. It's fascinating. I remember when Urban Artifact was announced. I thought, "That's badass," but also, "How?" because people weren't attuned to it.

BRET: That's the beauty of fruit. It's naturally acidic, so marrying fruit with tart helps people wrap their heads around it. Otherwise, it's just an uphill battle.

MIKE: To bring things back around to Rivertown, you were getting more involved in the business around the expansion, roughly 2015–16?

LINDSEY: Yeah, neither Jason nor I really had any identified roles. We just did whatever needed to be done. Obviously, Jason is brilliant when it comes to making beer, formulation and equipment—that kind of stuff. My skill set is trying to bring people together and create community, as well as how things look and feel, building the team and hiring, all the warm, fuzzy stuff.

Looking back, success through expansion was based on a number of things happening in a very specific way, and life happens. Nothing is guaranteed, and every single one of those specific things went totally awry. Nothing hurts more than when you invest hundreds of thousands of dollars in equipment and it does not work. Our brewhouse was great, but we really expanded the bottling line to help facilitate a lot of the contract brewing that we were doing.

BRET: That's a big piece of equipment.

LINDSEY: Yes, like a whole room. Huge. Yes, and parts of the entire line—with the exception of the filler from Pepsi that was from the '80s or '70s that worked great—did not work right. I also learned that yeast is completely unpredictable and on its own schedule. So, I had my nice spreadsheet made with this batch going out, then this batch here, then we'll go here and this will be great, and it never worked out like that. Jason had so many distractions dealing with manufacturers that were not supporting what they sold, and that's stressful when you have 50 million other things going on. So, it was wild, but we did it eventually. I don't think some of the production equipment ever worked right, not the way that it should have. And we also opened the restaurant. We had the ribbon cutting, and there were around four hundred to five hundred people. It was so exciting. Then all these people just walked in and sat down, and we realized that we hadn't thought about that, how the kitchen and the servers would handle four to five hundred people being seated at once. We got through it, but it was unexpected because we hadn't run a restaurant before. While we were opening the business, I also got pregnant with our second daughter.

BRET: You make an interesting point about how when you grow your business, you make these strategic decisions that are predicated on the steps you're going to take, the investments you're going to make and the risks that you're willing to take, and it's crazy. I often look at our own business at times and think—just one little misstep could bring it all down. As an entrepreneur, whether you consciously realize it or not, you're always under a lot of pressure, and when the leaders are in tough spaces, it's hard for the whole rest of the team too. That has really hit me over the last eight years of running this brewery—how much of an impact an owner and leader of a company has on the attitude and emotional well-being of everyone else.

LINDSEY: Oh, it's wild. In fact, I was recently at this conference where one of the speakers was saying that leaders can impact their team's mental well-being around 68 percent, the same amount as a spouse. For reference, they said a therapist impacts your mental health like 1 percent. That's heavy to think about. I'm very grateful for the time that I had with Jason, and we have amazing kids, but we weren't necessarily the best match. I think about being married and having two very different views about how to go about things, even though we were working towards the same goal. We just had two very different paths. That must have been stressful for him because I know it was stressful for me. I just wanted to make things work, and I think there were different times where maybe I pushed too hard. That was probably a misstep of mine, instead of being like, "OK, you lead, I'll follow," it was two very strong leaders trying to do things in two very different ways. I don't think that was a tension that brought the business down, but I think it was one that was probably tough on the mental health for the team.

MIKE: What is an example of your differences in approach to the business?

LINDSEY: Well, I have been blessed with a naturally optimistic personality. I've also been blessed with the ability to see the human in front of me, even when people are doing real horrible shit. I have the ability to step back and see that you're probably doing real horrible shit because you are hurting right now, and what you need is connection, but you have a very dysfunctional way of going about it. So, I go with the flow. We can overcome this, everything will be cool. I think Jason has had it reinforced enough times in his life that it's hard for him to trust people, especially with your dream and things that are important. With the expansion into Monroe, there were so many things that reinforced that he can't trust people, like all the problems with manufacturers. So, I'd be over here rallying the team, and Jason is on fire struggling in production. I don't necessarily think that one way is better or worse than the other, but I think it's important to have a balance.

BRET: How did you go from dipping your toes in the Rivertown water to being sucked into becoming the CEO?

LINDSEY: When we opened in December 2017, my aunt was dealing with cancer. She had gotten better; then she got sick again. My mom and her were living in Vegas. I had a feeling, so I decided to surprise my mom and aunt and just go out there for three days. At this point, our youngest daughter was nine months old. Long story short, I ended up being out there for two weeks, and my aunt passed. That was a life-changing experience on a bunch of different levels. I went back to work a couple weeks after, and we would wear the baby around the brewery. Jason said, "I have to go back into focusing on production, and I know everything is a cluster, but I really think that if there is an opportunity for this business to change, you have that capability," and he asked me if I would act in the role of CEO. My gut said no, but then my ego crept in and was like, "Oh, but you can show everybody how you can turn this all around, prove everyone wrong. How cool would that be? Rivertown will rise from the ashes, and it will be so great." So, I said yes. I bought like bright-red lipstick, and I was like a boss bitch. The number one thing that I would have done differently—and I don't necessarily think it would have changed the outcome—I would have asked for help three months sooner than I did, but I just had in my mind, "I can fix this! I can fix this!" I was meeting with investors. I made some changes with the contract brewing work that we were doing, which wasn't profitable, then the equipment issues on top.

MIKE: I've always thought of contract brewing as one of the more profitable things a brewery could do?

LINDSEY: It can be. The reason why contract brewing made sense was because it provided extra volume that allowed us to buy in bulk. The Rivertown brand, like the cases and the carriers, all benefited from the extra quantity that we could get. That made the Rivertown brand more profitable. Contract brewing is interesting in this case because there was not a contract. That was issue number one. They gave us projections. Then we made the beer and said, "Come pick it up," but they constantly changed the projections. There were all kinds of red flags. I remember sitting down and seeing that this is why we're losing money on this. It makes my heart sad, but everything that possibly could have went wrong went wrong. The contract people that we were working with were really big, like huge. It was when there were all the fires in California that affected wine, and one of their wineries was impacted. So, while there was money coming in from these contracts, they were not paying on time, and these are six-figure invoices. That's hard.

Bret, Lindsey and Mike at the *Brew Skies* studio bar. *Courtesy of Dan Phenicie.*

MIKE: "They weren't paying them on time" means that you were floating all that cash and material expenses?

LINDSEY: Correct, and the projections would change. The expansion into Monroe was based on several things working out a certain way, and contract brewing was one of them.

MIKE: That should have been a guaranteed base income.

LINDSEY: Right, in theory.

MIKE: I'm a lawyer. We should have met a few years ago, and I would have explained the contract part of contract brewing.

LINDSEY: I know, right? I was surprised too. Jason is so great at very small details, so the nebulousness of the agreement was surprising to me. So, that was one decision, to end the contract brewing, because it was money, but it was bad money. That was going on, and currently in our country, breweries can't just switch their distributors.

BRET: It's ridiculous. It's ridiculous bullshit.

LINDSEY: Yes, it's a ridiculous situation. We had switched distributors once, and we wanted to switch distributors. We were experiencing what is very normal in the beer industry. You're with a distributor, everything is hunky-dory and they do everything they can. Then you become just one of a myriad of their brands.

BRET: And they get a huge cut.

LINDSEY: Oh my gosh, it's ridiculous. At the time, we had an incredible sales team. Since I had been with Heidelberg and had that relationship, we wanted to switch distributors. We switched from Stagnaro to Heidelberg, the AB division specifically, because they did not have a lot of craft brands. They didn't have any local craft brands, and I had the relationship. Then Heidelberg was not doing a great job because the distributor side of the beer business needs to be completely revamped because it is not working for anyone except the distributors.

BRET: Distributors are doing great because it's a pretty low-risk game to be a completely unnecessary middleman.

LINDSEY: There came a time with Heidelberg where it sucked so bad that we had sold ninety-six new placements, and they delivered two of them.

MIKE: You sold ninety-six new accounts and they only delivered two of them?

LINDSEY: Yes.

MIKE: Holy shit!

LINDSEY: Our sales team was out there hustling, and it was clearly a failure of the distributor to perform.

BRET: Yeah. Did you invite them in to discuss it, or did you just call them a lot of names?

LINDSEY: There was a lot of discussion. I feel like we did everything that we could. I understand that everybody has to do what's best for their business, but it was choking ours. It got to a point where I made a phone call—because I know these people—and I told them, "If this does not change, we are about two months away from closing our doors. I am asking you to please let us self-distribute because it is the only thing that may be able to save us." I would send pictures of empty shelves and say, "Just let us go. Nobody else wants us anyway; just let us try to have a go at it." So, everything went silent, then they wanted us to buy out the contract. I'm like, "Dudes, we are two months away from closing our doors. I don't have the money." Long story short, we ended up getting out of it, and I feel very proud about it. You're in a powerful place when you literally have nothing to lose. One of the very last conversations was like, "All right, if you do not release us from our contract and we close our doors, make sure you understand that I will tell absolutely everybody—everybody!—in the beer industry that will listen that the reason we closed our doors is because you would not let us self-distribute and you prevented us from being able to move our business forward." I don't know if it was necessarily the thing that did it, but it was helpful. We self-distributed, and we did our best. It was very old school. Something that was beautiful about Rivertown was this very tenacious attitude. Let's figure it out.

BRET: Good for you, because when you boil it down, the system is set up to give 100 percent of the power to the distributors.

LINDSEY: Yes, they're not contractually obligated to use best efforts to move your product, but you're locked into a one-sided marriage that you can't get out of. It was originally done to protect distributors because there used to be ten thousand distributors and three hundred breweries. Now, it's flipped, but the laws are still in place to protect the distributors.

BRET: Which sucks for everybody but distributors, and the fact that they can treat us like playing cards, and they can sell our brands to other distributors or make us pay—it's just insane.

LINDSEY: Yeah, and it makes me sad—being an old, jaded beer person—when I see these new breweries pop up, and I see them join with a distributor. And I picture them feeling very similar to the way I'm sure you felt when you first went with a distributor. Like, this is gonna be great! They're a big name, and they're gonna distribute my product everywhere. I can mark selling off my calendar for the next five days.

MIKE: When you look at the success of Rhinegeist, there are multiple reasons for their success, but timing and that decision to self-distribute are two of the big ones, and they're connected in their case. At the time you had like four people walking into a bar in a week to sell beer. You had somebody from each distributorship, and you had somebody from Rhinegeist. That's a different world from Rivertown starting self-distributorship in 2018. At that point, there's a lot of breweries self-distributing because they have to, because the distributor doesn't even want more breweries at this point—not small craft brands. You were in a world where a Rivertown rep is walking into a bar to approach a bar manager that is surly and pissed off because there are twenty-five people lined up to sell that person their beer. What was that like?

LINDSEY: I'm still amazed and still feel an immense gratitude for our crazy team. What we did?

MIKE: A lot of cocaine?

LINDSEY: Definitely not cocaine, more good vibes. We built a sales team that just didn't give a fuck. They were scrappy. It was stressful for everyone, but we had fun with it and we did the best that we could. It's the relationship building, and it helped us stand out that we had some really cool, innovative liquid coming out at that point. And Rivertown was still a storied name.

MIKE: If this were fiction, this would be the start of a heroic comeback story. Unfortunately, the wheels came off instead. What happened?

LINDSEY: At one point, I got really sick because of stress, living on French fries and not sleeping. In November 2018, I was in the hospital twice in a week with this crazy headache. I could barely talk, and I remember trying to work on a spreadsheet to show an investor, and there was drama going on with the boiler. I remember walking into Rivertown the smallest version of myself possible, trying to shuffle in to sit at this meeting with my lawyer and Jason and the dudes from the boiler place. And my lawyer was like, "Why are you here?" But I felt like I needed to be there to help facilitate the conversation because there was so much tension, and I had this wicked migraine so bad that I'm in the hospital. I've always been somebody that believes that we should build a great, natural foundation with our bodies, then see what we need from there, and I definitely wasn't doing that. Coming out of that meeting, I remember Jason saying to me, "I think you need to check out some medicine," because I had some autoimmune diagnosis in 2017. He said, "I think you need to stop trying to do this on your own, because

I don't want to be wheeling you around in a wheelchair at our daughter's graduation." That's where the change started to happen. Jason took over more of the executive stuff, and as my body started to heal, I started seeing things differently in my life. I started to see that some of the things going on in my life were not in alignment. Then, September 2019, Jason and I split, and that was the end of my tenure in Rivertown.

I think part of what made Rivertown a storied brewery is the tenacity of the people that worked there, and their dedication. Looking back, it was way too much to ask of anyone, but everybody stepped up and did the best that they could. I'm not exactly sure what happened after I left, but I can say with full confidence that Jason and the team that was there did everything that they possibly could. I think that when COVID hit, everything was highly reliant on taproom sales, and again, everything that could go wrong went wrong. Who would have predicted a pandemic would hit at a time of really limited resources? That's a crazy unknown.

MIKE: That takes me back to Rhinegeist for contrast. Those guys have run a very good business and they've made good decisions, but they're also a company that luck has always shined on. Everything that could have gone right there went right.

LINDSEY: Rhinegeist is really interesting to me. If I go back to the Goose Island days, we started Cincinnati Beer Week. It's a collaborative thing. Before Rhinegeist came around, everybody was very collaborative with each other. That still goes on, but I pick up more of a guardedness. Before Rhinegeist, it was like, "Sure, let me give you my recipe, this is how I troubleshot it, here's some grain." When I started out here, there were five local breweries. Now, there's a bajillion of them, so there are multiple reasons, but I feel like when Rhinegeist came along, they changed the whole culture of Cincinnati beer. It went from "We're in this together" to "Oh, you can't fuck around anymore." Rhinegeist came in with very well-funded marketing, the liquid was good and they had real business acumen.

MIKE: They were far better capitalized than anybody had been.

LINDSEY: Yes, absolutely. Back in 2005, when I got into beer, it was good enough if you had a passion for making beer and you made decent-tasting beer. Then, by 2009, 2010, 2011, the quality of the liquid became more important, and you needed to start some marketing. By the time Rhinegeist came along, you needed to have quality marketing and business acumen to be successful. Then Rhinegeist brought some big boy tactics to the local market. It's kind of a cold feeling. You know what I mean? It's been interesting to watch them grow, but I feel like they changed the culture. Cincinnati Beer Week was the canary in the coal mine. People loved it. It grew, and then, within the span of two years, it was just gone. The first years that I was involved, it felt very collaborative, community-oriented. It was not just about beer specials. We were going to educate people, celebrate well-crafted beer together as a community and what we have going on here. As it grew, there came a point when I had to step down because people's egos and selfish intentions flooded in, and it turned into something different than its original intention. That was the demise of Beer Week. There are times when I wonder if it would be possible to do something like that again. It was a really cool experience.

BRYANT GOULDING

How Rhinegeist Took Over the World

Rhinegeist is a brewery that needs little introduction to Cincinnatians. A modern icon, a monolith of Cincinnati beer culture, up there with the Cincinnati gastronomic elites like Skyline Chili and Graeter's Ice Cream. The true beauty of Rhinegeist is, well, the beauty of Rhinegeist! Specifically, its graphic design, the taproom experience and its desire to give people what they want: fun.

◆ ◆ ◆

MIKE: I think you're from Northern California, so how did you wind up in Over-the-Rhine, which, at the time, was the shittiest neighborhood in a random Midwest city?

BRYANT: I have Bob Bonder [Bryant's business partner and co-founder of Rhinegeist] to thank for finding Cincinnati. Bob and I met in San Francisco as consultants where we were both following our passions. His was home roasting coffee and making amazing lattes, and mine was homebrewing beer, which I fell in love with when studying abroad in London, where I learned to see beer as a vehicle for social connection. There was one particular pub, a Fuller's Pub, that used to be the old Bank of England. There was so much marble in that place, and so many businessmen in suits. They were coming together, having pints, doing serious business and enjoying themselves while they did it. This marriage between alcohol, business and the real world became foundational for me. When I came back to the United States—I still wasn't twenty-one—I bought Charlie Papazian's book, *A New Complete Joy of Home Brewing*, and I started brewing batches in my backyard. I ended up with a lot of knowledge and understanding, mostly that I couldn't make the quality of beer that I liked to drink!

I eventually got my hands on a copy of *Brewing Up a Business* by Sam Calagione, and I read it in an afternoon. Brewing seemed like a fun way to make a living if you could. Fast-forward to me getting a job at Accenture, which allowed me to get a taste of the corporate world and how dissatisfying it was. So, I quit my job in consulting and got a job in craft beer.

Soon, Bob called me up and said, "You gotta come check Cincinnati out. They're drinking a ton of craft beer here, and we should build a brewery. I know a guy that brews at Rock Bottom. We could put this all together and make it happen." I was working for Dogfish Head, and I found selling beer to be really satisfying. You get to meet a lot of people, and you get to talk about the thing you love. You find the coolest parts of the coolest towns with the coolest people running the coolest pubs and restaurants. I found it all fascinating and fun, and there was no way I was moving from California to Ohio—until I came out to visit Cincinnati.

Cincinnati, and Over-the-Rhine in particular, really felt grounded with its ties to the great age of American industry, all the Italianate architecture and the scale of Over-the-Rhine. Bob charmed me with Cincinnati. He was pretty good at putting together a tour of all the interesting creatives in a five-hundred-yard radius, hitting the hippest bars and driving around kind of wistfully imagining what it was like in its heyday. We saw a city that had so much character that I had underestimated. I flew home, and the visit sat with me. I realized that this was an amazing opportunity to move up in the sales world. I didn't really have the experience to put me in a position of power and autonomy, and I knew that. I didn't have the confidence either. But my exposure to other brands and different markets gave me hope that this was possible.

MIKE: Your early exposure to beer in England, in fantastic pubs full of suits and marble, is in stark contrast to where I grew up in Appalachian Ohio. For me, beer was this yellow watery thing that we pounded a whole bunch of for the express purpose of getting drunk. I discovered craft beer as a young adult, but it sounds like you developed a much more romantic view of beer from the beginning.

Bryant Goulding makes the first delivery of a Rhinegeist keg. It went to the Lackman, an Over-the-Rhine bar on Vine Street. *Courtesy of Rhinegeist Brewing Company.*

BRYANT: Yeah, I mean, in high school we would get thirty-packs of whatever from whomever would buy them for us. So, that phase briefly existed.

BRET: It's interesting that you realized that you weren't able to brew the beers that you wanted to drink early on. That level of self-reflection and insight is rare in the craft beer world. It ties into your romanticism as well. Being able to see Cincinnati and the bones that were there when you guys were first looking at the city, allowing you to see the potential.

BRYANT: Bob and I knew we weren't going to be the brewers. That put us on a path to find Jim Matt [Rhinegeist's original head brewer], and I'm really glad we did. We began looking for a place for our brewery. We were looking at old nineteenth-century breweries, several places, including the Jackson Brewery building. Then we went into the building that became the brewery that we're in now, and it was like 200,000 square feet! That was way too much space. We just wanted to see it because it was an old brewery. We wanted to come to Cincinnati to be a part of this tapestry of legit pre-Prohibition breweries that built this city. The opportunity felt really rich. I felt like we could build this thing. People love beer in Cincinnati. They have since Cincinnati existed. So, we got the building that we were sure was too big, and we started to put together a brewery.

The original owner of our brewery building, Christian Moerlein, was brewing 300,000 barrels—three times what we're doing in the brewery now. And most of that was sold in Cincinnati! That is an astounding amount of beer for the population of that time. We wanted to pay homage and respect to the history, but we knew we were gonna brew modern beers. We wanted to be progressive. We wanted to brew the beers we wanted to make. IPA is what craft beer was built on, more or less.

So yeah, I guess that's what I saw.

MIKE: You give your partner, Bob, the credit for your decision to move to Cincinnati. But once upon a time, you told me that on your flight back to San Francisco from your first visit here, you read my first book, *Over-the-Rhine: When Beer Was King*, and that I was the reason that you decided to come to Cincinnati and start Rhinegeist and become incredibly successful. So, my real question is, where is my check, Bryant!?

BRYANT: Good question. Good question. No, I think you're a valuable contributor though. The preservation and the respect and the love of the history of Cincinnati is more prominent in all of Cincinnati than what I was experiencing in San Francisco. In Cincinnati, it's so distinct and so much a part of life here because it's been so well preserved, especially in OTR.

MIKE: But it was raw. You could definitely see the history, but the celebration of history wasn't accidental. When I started promoting Over-the-Rhine around 2005, people didn't even recognize those buildings as having been brewery buildings. But you're right, what was fantastic, what was unique about Cincinnati in 2010, was that so much of Over-the-Rhine was still in terrible disrepair, but it was there, still standing. You could see the history all around you.

BRYANT: Yeah, two thoughts. One, anytime I told people I was moving to Cincinnati for this opportunity, they scoffed at it because they'd never been here. Then they'd come visit and be bowled over by how charming it is. The second is that Bob would hear you, Mike, as a tour guide outside of his window telling the story of Cincinnati brewery history. And he was like, "There's no modern local brewery here." Your tours solidified in our minds the opportunity in Cincinnati to be a part of a brewing revival.

Growing up in Connecticut, everything's boring. Now, as an adult, I go back and I love it. But it was boring. And when I went out to California, it was like living in Technicolor. It's vivid, it's creative. You can't open up a coffee shop and have it be the same as the other coffee shop down the street. It's gotta have its own angle. And that level of competition and creativity was really stimulating. I felt like we could bring some of that to Cincinnati.

MadTree opened up six months before us. They kind of had their team built. But as we grew in parallel, we picked up a lot of people from other industries. The level of talent we were able to get was outsized versus other breweries. That's one of the things that has been fundamental to our success. And Bret, you brought that up. We knew we weren't going do everything. We knew we had to delegate and scale. When we built Rhinegeist, we learned that we can lead and we can set up a framework, but we can't do it ourselves. We picked up a lot of people from landscapers to chemists and put a team together. More than half of our people have been here for over five years. That kind of retention, even as a lot of breweries have opened up around us, has been a testament to our ability to hire the right people and mostly get out of their way.

BRET: The learning-to-delegate skill—it's crazy how important that is. It feels like you can keep grinding and grinding forever, but you can't. At some point, your body says, "No, I'm not doing this anymore."

You're not from Cincinnati, and we all know that Cincinnati loves Cincinnati. It's very guarded about all things not from Cincinnati. How the hell did you get the city to buy into you guys and Rhinegeist as wholeheartedly as it has?

BRYANT: I was an outsider for sure. In San Francisco, it was a city of outsiders. Cincinnati is not. I mean, I've been dreaming about this for a decade, right? I'm selling beer, but I'm dreaming about owning a brewery, not actually thinking that I could ever do it. I've got the people side covered. I can run around like a puppy dog and tell everybody about the thing that

The Rhinegeist crew in 2019, in their massive taproom. Founders Bryant Goulding and Bob Bonder are seated in the middle. *Courtesy of Rhinegeist Brewing Company.*

I'm excited about. Bob can raise the money and make sure that we are profitable. There are some real synergies here—this could work. Selling beer for Dogfish Head, I spent five years cracking into cities that I didn't live in. I'd sleep on my buddy's couch in Ocean Beach in San Diego and try and win them over on Dogfish. I had a brand from Delaware, and San Diego didn't need IPA from Delaware—but I found the spots. And I think I did the same thing here in Cincinnati.

Kenny and Brady, the co-founders of MadTree, had me over for one of their Ping-Pong nights. And I drank their homebrew before they opened their brewery. I felt very welcomed in Cincinnati. When we pitched investors, where we became successful was finding those people that wanted Cincinnati to win, understood OTR's role in that and what a brewery could do.

MIKE: I was in Hawaii a couple years ago, and a bartender asked where I was from. I said Cincinnati, and the first word out of his mouth was *Rhinegeist*. It's amazing how far your reach has extended. Your success has been spectacular. But if you go back to 2013, you were early contemporaries with MadTree, operating on about the same scale. Currently, they're making great beers and they're doing well, but they're not doing Rhinegeist well. Bret and I sometimes philosophize about the different paths your breweries took. I don't want to put you on the spot, but we'd love to know your perspective on where the forks in the road were that set Rhinegeist on a path that went a different direction from MadTree.

BRYANT: I have a ton of respect for those guys. I know Brady and Kenny well, they run an awesome company and they've done things differently. I think on the structural side, we're both really talented organizations. So, there's mutual respect. People like rivalry, right? So, with MadTree and Rhinegeist growing up at the same time, you always heard the question, "Who do you like?" Well, do you like good beer? I know I do, and if Psychopathy is the IPA that's on tap, I'm gonna drink it. I like it. But I think what allowed us to hit escape velocity was our space, with the ability to plunk in new tanks. That and our initial business plan.

MadTree filled up their capacity. Then they were faced with a big question around how they were going to navigate their way to more space, whereas we were more streamlined. That is a fundamental piece of it. I respect those guys, but we did things differently. We still get beers together and enjoy each other's company and enjoy the fact that we've contributed to the culture of craft beer, and we put Cincinnati on the map. I mean, they're well respected, and they've traveled well too. Ultimately, I don't know, is it our name? Is it the fact that we have kind of a scary but not so scary that your mom won't wear the T-shirt logo?

BRET: The branding is not the sole reason, but that is part of the formula. Look at how many breweries in America now have what I would call a "Rhinegeist look" to them. Before you guys existed, that look didn't exist. Cans with a one-third color stripe and two-thirds on top, logo centered on top. You see that everywhere now. Your beer, Truth, is almost like what an IPA can looks like now. It's copied at all sorts of other breweries. You have a visual look that's like the way that copying something became Xeroxing or searching on the internet became Googling it. And in a market that was already saturated and already had so many craft breweries in it, that's just goddamn impressive.

BRYANT: I think that our design was a part of our success. Always making consistently good beer is huge, obviously. But standing out on the shelf is too. I think another major contributing factor, that I don't wanna gloss over, is our decision to self-distribute. You pick up so much control, you can be aggressive but with the detail of a scalpel. We weren't delivering draft beer beyond what we could service. We have had Truth pouring in the same bars since July of 2013. That's such an honor that they continue to choose our brand. It is also a testament to our customer service and our intentionality. A level of intentionality we would not have gotten by adding a distributor who has their own thoughts and ideas on how to treat your brand.

MIKE: Where did you come up with the idea of self-distributing? Was that a model that you had seen work elsewhere?

BRYANT: There were a handful of breweries whose products were vaporizing anytime it hit shelves, and they all self-distributed. Brian Hunt from Moonlight drove a Sprinter van around making deliveries. He brewed the beer, he kegged the beer and then he delivered the beer. I thought it was incredible that this sixty-year-old He-Man was delivering kegs to all the crazy basements in San Francisco. I would see him, as I would be out drinking a beer at the bar, dropping his kegs off with a smile on his face. He's why we have Sprinter vans. Bob was originally dismissive of self-distribution. It seemed like a lot of hard work. And it is a lot of hard work, but Bob heard something from Omar, the owner of Sun King Brewery. He said, "What's

The choice to self-distribute as the local craft beer industry was just starting to explode in 2012 is one of the multiple reasons for Rhinegeist's success. *Courtesy of Rhinegeist Brewing Company.*

the worst thing that can happen? You build up your brand, and then you sell it to someone better equipped to take it to the next level." The exposure we had to the world of craft beer outside of Cincinnati allowed us to bring in best practices to a city that was ready to embrace quality and creativity in their beer.

MIKE: It was exciting when Rhinegeist first opened. You guys were a transformative part of the redevelopment of Over-the-Rhine at the time.

BRYANT: I think it was July 7, 2012, Washington Park opened up right at the same time we started brewing. Our neighborhood, Over-the-Rhine, was teeming with people celebrating this park and the growth of our city. It was a beautiful day, and it felt like fifty businesses in OTR all opened at the same time. We were broadcasting this message of urban revitalization wider than the other businesses in OTR could because beer travels. We were telling this story of urban renewal with our liquid. This story of the rebirth of beer to a city of beer lovers, with respect to the history of beer that built this city to begin with. I get goosebumps still talking about it, ten years in.

MIKE: How integral to your early vision of the brewery was the taproom, with the changes that occurred in Ohio in 2012 that legalized taprooms? Until then, taprooms didn't exist as we know them today. When 2012 hit, every brewery that was already in existence had to figure out how to cobble on a taproom. Whereas you guys opened with this incredible building and a taproom that was twenty times the size of anything anybody else had. Was the size of the taproom an important part of your original business plan?

BRYANT: No, we completely underestimated it because we hadn't seen it done. And the neighborhood, you know, we were comfortable, but like…

MIKE: Yeah, it was a hard sell to get people to go to Over-the-Rhine at the time.

BRYANT: You're walking past prostitutes, that we eventually got to know, and were a part of the neighborhood. But on a daily basis, there was crime and there were reasons why people were a little bit scared. Things have improved, but originally it was just gonna be the production space without a taproom. We completely underestimated the importance of our taproom because it didn't seem that big of a deal. In hindsight, there's just so few indoor spaces like ours. I mean, you gotta go to Venice to a cathedral to feel that much open space, or a convention center, which is not the same punch viscerally.

MIKE: Yeah, it's a nice combination of historic and industrial. The area where you have the primary bar, that's a cool little section of the building. I always wondered why that part of the building was so ornate for originally being a factory. In doing research a few years back, I learned that Christian Moerlein was going to build an event space shortly before Prohibition. They were going to hold private events on the second floor of their bottling room, where they'd have a big beer fountain, beautiful decorations, et cetera. They built the space out, but Prohibition hit and it was never used for its original purpose—until Rhinegeist happened to put your main taproom bar there.

BRYANT: That is a major mystery solved for us! We never understood why. And that's awesome to picture that kind of use unknowingly being passed down one hundred years later.

The Rhinegeist Brewery, Over-the-Rhine, Cincinnati. *Courtesy of Rhinegeist Brewing Company.*

BRET: Do you think that you guys were doing things a little bit differently than everybody else operating at the time?

BRYANT: When we started, I was leading our sales organization, which was only a handful of us. We had 8:00 a.m. Friday morning meetings every week.

BRET: Oh, Jesus.

BRYANT: And I held them on Friday mornings because I knew myself and most of the team were a pretty social bunch. If it wasn't 8:00 a.m., you were going to stay out an hour later the night before because we don't run sales routes on Fridays. And we don't sell or deliver on Saturday either. So, Friday at the 8:00 a.m. meeting, everyone grumbled about, but it was a level of discipline that we had that others didn't. We can't just party all the time. It has to be business. That's actually one of the things that comes up when you talk to people about Rhinegeist. That combination of it being a good place to work, but also that we brought a degree of professionalism to the local brewing scene that wasn't there before.

BRET: To me, I think you can still find the family within craft beer, and you can certainly still find the party animals. But with the market tightening up, it seems like the competition side of craft beer is starting to come out a little bit more compared to ten years ago.

BRYANT: The number of craft breweries is just bigger. You go to craft brewers' conferences, and you don't know as many people. The scale has become more challenging to create tight bonds. I forget the law, but you can have like 150 personal connections—and no human can have more than that. And that's not even speaking of friends. Real friends are probably closer to 5. Because of those numbers, it is really competitive.

BRET: I don't even like 150 people.

BRYANT: It's really competitive in sales, but if you have an issue in brewing, no matter who you are in Cincinnati, we're going to help you out. There's so much camaraderie on the production side. We respect each other. And I think that's really special in our industry.

BRET: What's the first great beer you had? What's the first beer that turned you on to how truly great beer can taste, that it can be more than just light lager?

BRYANT: There's three beers for me that opened my eyes. One is London Pride, the first legal beer I had while flying alone as an eighteen-year-old to London. They were serving London Pride in cans, and most good beer wasn't in cans at that time in 2000. The second was Rodenbach, a Flanders Red. My first sip, I thought, "What the hell is this!? This is nonsense." But I came to really love that sour beer style. The third foundational beer for me was Stone IPA. I cracked a can of Stone IPA open, and it was this bouquet of tropical fruit. I never experienced anything like that beer before. It was West Coast IPA incarnate.

MIKE: How sad is it that Stone Brewing is now owned by Sapporo?

BRYANT: I don't know how to feel anymore about that. I've softened on my stance around selling out because I don't know what to make of it. I'm forty-two today and I have gas left in the tank now, but what about at fifty-two, or sixty-two or even seventy-two? I'm going to feel differently.

Independence is something that means so much to us doing craft beer. But the consumer has proven that they don't care if they're independent or owned by Anheuser-Busch. They just don't. That's the reality of it. So, like, the customer is never wrong.

BRET: Then, as an industry of independent craft brewers, do we cut them out because now they're a global corporate brand?

BRYANT: They're still all the same people with the same knowledge and the same generous hearts. That camaraderie is there. If we choose to stay small and to stay scrappy, we are also choosing to stay less strong and resilient. What does craft beer even mean? We're independent, we're craft, but if that doesn't matter to the consumer, what does that all even mean? And I don't know that I have as much of a problem with it as I did, but independence was so formative to our brand. It was my stance. But once again, that's my perspective at forty-two. At thirty-two, I was like, "Hell no! Fuck those guys!" But now the lines are so blurred, what's the point?

MIKE: I understand what both of you are saying, but as somebody that's not in the industry I need to say this. First, the consumer is wrong almost all the fucking time. Second, what I have seen with some of these beers is that the quality never really seems to stay the same after selling out. This conversation with you sounds very similar to a conversation that we had with Fritz Maytag, the founder of Anchor Brewing. Fritz was talking about his view of the importance of independence changing and the idea of going public as being part of a company's evolution. Even selling out to Sapporo was just a part of the natural evolution. He said it wasn't going to change the beer. All of it was logical, and everything he said was heartfelt. Then, within a year of selling out, Sapporo decided to completely dismantle America's first craft brewery. When you get to that level of corporate money, it's inevitable that you lose the soul. People just quit giving a shit about the relationship between a brewery and its communities and its own history.

BRYANT: I know a lot of people in San Francisco that partied until the lights went out at Anchor Brewing. That's one of the first breweries I visited when I first visited San Francisco. They literally partied in that beautiful place 'til the lights went out. I saw it on Instagram, just living vicariously through them. It sucks but I just care about people at the end of the day. Consolidation happens because of capitalism. We're on this conveyor belt.

Profit is necessary. You have to play that game. Some of us are better at running businesses than others. With ten thousand breweries in the U.S., I think we're going to see more and more consolidation. I think creative destruction does happen, and I'm just watching and trying to figure it all out.

BRET: That's all we all can do in life. Just try to figure things out. Speaking of figuring things out, what was the thing about running Rhinegeist that took you most by surprise?

BRYANT: We didn't expect the amount of awareness that we could generate with $0 in marketing. We touched on a nerve that was this pride in local beer. We are a beer-loving city. We opened in late June, and after about six months, we were out of stock and almost never caught up. That was something that I didn't expect at all. Also, it's hard to keep your hand on the rudder of company culture. We went from ten to fifty thousand barrels of beer production in three years. That was really hard on a team that we didn't hire enough of. What was unexpected for us at the time was how much people can scale, but you can get burned out quickly, and it's hard to find that balance. We lost some good people that we pushed too hard. Not because that was our intention, but because scaling is challenging.

BRET: What was your happiest moment in craft beer so far?

BRYANT: I cried the most when I walked in on our tenth anniversary, and we had created this awesome museum of brand reflection. I really love the times when my friends win awards—we won an award for Sherry Ink. That was an amazing moment when we won a Great American Beer Festival medal, where the odds are so against you. That's a pretty proud moment. I really liked the first night we opened our taproom. We had two thousand people show up, and we ran out of one-dollar bills. My dad and brother had to run to the casino to get more! It was all-hands-on-deck, with my whole family helping. We only had seven employees at the time, and two thousand people came through! That was really gratifying. There have been so many moments like that with our team.

BRET: Are you noticing that as Rhinegeist is aging, over ten years old is a good bit of time, that your customer base is continuing to expand in that you're bringing in Gen Z and new drinkers to Rhinegeist?

People enjoying great beers and views from the Rhinegeist rooftop deck. *Courtesy of Rhinegeist Brewing Company.*

BRYANT: The risk of brewing at our scale is you tend to get numb to innovation. We can't float along with the people that fell in love with us ten years ago because as they age, we'll render ourselves out of customers. Things like Cincy Light [a beer brewed with Cincy Reigns, the University of Cincinnati NIL collective] help us plug into the emergent Gen Z college drinker. A lot of people love the University of Cincinnati. It's an emergent brand, team and institution. We're always thinking about how we refresh as we age. And staying relevant is one of those things where there is no magic potion. You can't stay stagnant and be the coolest brand forever. You have to stretch and keep your core strong and have a good diet. And those are the types of things where company culture, staying attuned to trends and being aware of your demographics matters. We look to other brands outside of beer as well. We're always attuned to the trends out there in design, the waves out there of culture and sentiment. We have a beer brand called Truth that's ten years old, and we haven't had to do much with it. The name says a lot without using too many words. We're trying to keep that in mind, that a brand like Truth is hard to come by in this day and age. Truth, for Rhinegeist, is a calm in the storm, at least for a moment. You can crack open a can and just kind of escape to the connection that we have with each other. It stands

162

for something to us. It's kind of like the definition of pornography—you know it when you see it. Staying true to our core, controlling what we can control and making sure we're still having fun.

BRET: Any final advice for us Bryant?

BRYANT: Thinking about the balance of life: keep it fun, keep it relevant, but build an architecture around keeping the core strong. I think that works in life and our portfolio of beers at Rhinegeist.

❖ ❖ ❖

Rhinegeist is a capitalist fairy tale: An outsider to the city sees opportunity for growth and development in a fledgling cottage industry. They buy a run-down historic building and bring it back to life. Their brand and logo become city icons, traveling from coast to coast. Truth becomes the number one IPA in the state of Ohio, and their status as Cincinnati legends grows. The neighborhood they're in goes from blight to bright. It seems like the only thing that can stop this brewery is if it loses its company soul—or sells out.

URBAN ARTIFACT

Learning that the Customer Is Always Right, Even When They're Wrong

The customer is always right. It's a phrase we've all heard repeated ad nauseam, usually by the local Karen as they berate an underpaid retail worker. This, however, is wrong. The real phrase is "The customer is always right, in matters of what sells." The difference is that the customer knows very little about most things, but they know exactly what they want. They might not be able to tell you why it's good or bad, but they'll definitely tell you if they love it or hate it. This key difference was a hard lesson to learn for Bret, but the effects it has had on Urban Artifact have been undeniable. It's part of how Urban Artifact became America's largest all-fruit brewery.

◆ ◆ ◆

MIKE: It surprised me that you didn't start drinking until a relatively responsible age.

BRET: Yeah, I waited until I graduated high school, the summer between high school and college. So still, you know, illegal but relatively responsible.

MIKE: Not drinking in high school is a crazy concept to me because I graduated at the end of the drunken, debaucherous 1980s. What was the high school scene like for you as a millennial?

BRET: It wasn't until my junior year that I even saw alcohol at a party. Granted, I was a giant dork for my first two years of high school. I still am, of course, but giant dorks don't normally get invited to those kinds of parties.

MIKE: You were drinking by your freshman year at Ohio University, which is something we have in common—going to OU and drinking our way through—but we've been doing the *Brew Skies Happy Hour* podcast, Missing Linck Festival and earlier projects for over seven years now, and I just learned that you got suspended from OU for drunkenness.

BRET: At OU, if you get in trouble enough times, apparently you get suspended from school. I got busted for underage consumption in the dorm. I was fermenting my own wine in our dorm closet and selling it to dorm mates.

MIKE: Smart!

BRET: Another time, we were curiously wandering around a half-built building with drinks. The third time, I got busted for leaving a party and then falling asleep next to a stop sign in the grass. I wasn't hurt and I wasn't hurting anybody, but they took me to jail all the same. It was that third time that the school administration decided that I needed a break and made me take a semester off. I was a senior, one semester from graduating.

MIKE: Oh, good God. But that kind of worked out for you, right? You went out into the world and got an internship.

BRET: I knew I was getting suspended, so I started applying for co-ops and internships. I told prospective employers I was simply looking for an engineering co-op, not that I was getting suspended. Co-ops are a normal part of becoming an engineer, so it never raised any suspicions. I landed a role at Cargill, in Nebraska, finished that, went back to school and graduated a year later. It ended up being a great professional move.

MIKE: Were your parents thrilled?

BRET: Ha, no, definitely not. It was bad behavior. I was young and dumb. Hopefully I've learned a thing or two from the whole experience and am now a better person for it.

MIKE: The other big, unintentional career move you made in college was starting to homebrew.

BRET: Yes, homebrewing wine in our dorm led to homebrewing beer once we moved into a house off-campus. Homemade wine is great, but brewing beer is much cooler to an aspiring engineer in his early twenties. We brewed a couple batches, and they were bad.

MIKE: That's how most people start homebrewing, by making bad beer.

BRET: But if you stick it out you eventually brew a batch that's halfway decent. Then you're hooked. It quickly devolved into Scotty, now my business partner, and I brewing every weekend. We would start brewing at noon on Saturday, and we'd brew all afternoon, before heading out to party with our friends. That was life every weekend at OU until graduation.

MIKE: Aside from some misadventures, you were a relatively good college student. You got a degree as a chemical engineer and then went to work at Cargill.

BRET: Working as an engineer allowed me to learn that beer production isn't an art. It's far more a manufacturing process.

MIKE: What the hell does Cargill do? I know its food related and they're massive, but what do they do? And does it happen in a Death Star?

BRET: It's basically the Death Star, if the Death Star wore jeans and lived in Minneapolis. They are an agribusiness working within the food industry. They touch 33 percent of all the food that is made and consumed in America. From flour to dressings, to salt, juice and corn syrup. From protein to fertilizer. They're mindlessly, unfathomably large and soul-crushingly corporate. After four years, I'd had enough. The time had come to pursue my passion and open a craft brewery. In 2014, I quit and started Urban Artifact with my best friend and brew buddy, Scotty, and our new business partner, Scott Hand.

MIKE: What was the original business plan, and how did you guys think it through?

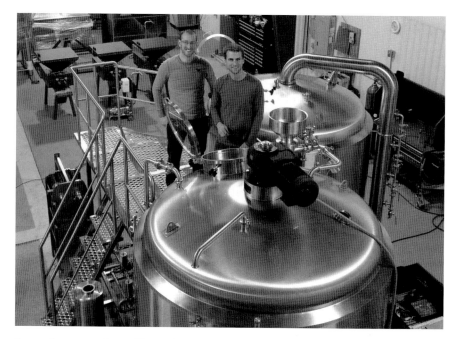

Bret and co-owner Scotty Hunter inspect their first brewing equipment before taking delivery. Take note of how dramatically Bret has aged from running a brewery. *Courtesy of Urban Artifact.*

BRET: We knew that we were already behind the eight ball. Craft beer was starting to roll, and we needed to differentiate ourselves. We were never going to beat Rhinegeist at marketing, nor could we outspend Christian Moerlein on their sales budget. We needed to create a niche for ourselves that others would struggle to copy. We looked at the oldest brands in the brewing world for inspiration. Brands like Guinness and Weinstephaner. The thing that stood out to us was that they did one thing, and they did that one thing better than any brewery in the world. Guinness with dry stout and Weinstephaner with hefeweizen. If we were going to succeed, we needed to aim for the same level of renown. Ultimately, we settled on fruit beer.

MIKE: You had a business plan and an idea. How did that result in buying an old church in Northside?

BRET: We narrowed down a list of ideal neighborhoods. Northside was at the top of our list. Then we just drove around, scoping out possible sites. We made a list of empty buildings to research with our realtor. There was one warehouse in Northside that I took an immediate shine to. Great location, lots of floor space, historic frontage and it looked completely empty. This warehouse, I would later tell my wife, Stephanie, would be freaking perfect. It's right next to a park. It's close to the main drag. We can make this an urban destination for anyone in Northside. We need to get that warehouse. The only issue might be that church across the street. What we didn't realize at the time was that we'd buy that church first and then expand into that warehouse later. Which I'm proud to say is exactly where my office is today.

MIKE: And you looked at Over-the-Rhine before that too, right?

BRET: Over-the-Rhine was the other big neighborhood we liked. We were looking at the old Jackson Brewery building. We had a deal in place to buy the property and renovate it with the help of a bank loan. In hindsight, with as much work as that building needed and as small as our loan was, we would have failed before we even opened our doors.

MIKE: A wonderful building that was in terrible shape.

BRET: Thankfully, the bank took one look at the property and said, "The walls are falling down, the foundation's crumbling, the roof is leaking and it's on an unstable hill. Everything about this choice of location is terrible. We're not giving you money for this building."

MIKE: Sometimes banks make good decisions. It's rare, but sometimes they're right. How did the deal at the church come about?

BRET: At the same time the bank was telling us we couldn't buy the Jackson Brewery, the church across the street from our ideal warehouse in Northside went up for sale. It was owned by a small cookie baking operation, Queen City Cookies. The rumor is that she sold her business to a large regional bakery and was looking to make a quick deal to get rid of the property. We swooped in, made an offer and closed the deal within two weeks.

MIKE: Didn't something happen with your business partner Scott Hand that almost brought the whole deal down?

BRET: Well, yes. Scott Hand had another business partner who was going to handle the brewing operations. They had their business planned, all their money lined out and the bank set up to close on their loan. The concept was great, actually: Craft Doughnuts and Craft Beer, a combination doughnut shop, brewery and taproom. However, two days before the loan closing, his brewer business partner calls him up and says, "Scott, I lost all my money."

MIKE: Like, on a bus or what?

BRET: Penny stocks.

MIKE: Well, his gamble led to you owning a church next to your and Scotty's ideal location. So, pretty serendipitous. You guys get opened in 2015, and your original business model included both sour and wild beers. Today, fruited sours are one of the fastest-growing styles in the U.S. What did the sour beer market look like in 2015? Did people get it?

BRET: No, no, no, it was not that. I will always remember the first week we were open, and an older gentleman walks in and loudly proclaims, "I heard y'all make sour beer here. Is that true? I heard that means it's spoiled." Which begs the question, "Well, good sir, why are you even here in the first place?" And the natural follow-up, "Since you're here, take a seat and let's try some sour beer." That happened a lot when we first started. The amount of people that came in and thought that we messed up brewing our beer was staggering. We learned over time that people actually love sour beer and tart flavors. People can get scared of new things, though, and what really helps people accept acidity in beer is fruit. By adding fruit to our beers, we were able to connect the flavor of our fruit tarts to a flavor experience that you have had when eating fresh fruit.

MIKE: It is interesting because Berliner weiss and gose are old traditional German beer styles, and Cincinnati is traditionally a German beer city. But the "German beer" in Cincinnati had become bad American adjunct-filled bastardizations of pilsners, and the history of German sour beer was lost locally. We had lost all that purposefully sour beer tradition over time. The only exposure Cincinnatians had to sour flavors in beer was when bacteria had infected the batch and it was, in fact, bad beer.

BRET: Yes, precisely. And it's a shame that I didn't realize when I was younger that the cultural heritage Cincinnati shares with Germany doesn't mean Cincinnatians will care about all things historically German. Our

The original Urban Artifact taproom crew on opening night. *Courtesy of Urban Artifact.*

logic that because sour beer had a historical significance to Germany meant that it could find modern cultural significance in Cincinnati was wrong.

MIKE: Early on, you made several sour beers and *Brettanomyces* beers that you couldn't get the public to understand. Phrenology was a good example. It was voted one of the best IPAs in America…

BRET: Eleventh best in 2018 according to *Paste* magazine.

MIKE: So, three years after you opened, you're making one of the top-rated beers in the United States, but it was a funky, wild IPA.

BRET: We put ourselves in a pickle early on because I didn't realize the importance of consumer expectations. If you're going to make a beer that has notes of horse blanket and barnyard hay in it, you better damn well do a good job of explaining the story of that beer. It is purposefully brewed to have funky flavors, and it's going to be a unique taste experience. I'm very, very proud of that recipe. But people didn't get it because I did a bad job of telling the story of that weird beer. It was a phenomenal beer. It just didn't sell for shit 'cause people didn't understand it.

MIKE: When I first started taking my UC students to Urban Artifact, you could find flavors here that you read on a beer flavor chart but that you can't wrap your head around until you taste them. They can be either positive flavors or off-flavors. Band-Aid is an off-flavor example. I used to read that and think, "Who knows what a Band-Aid tastes like?" Then I had a beer that had that off flavor, and I immediately recognized it. It's the same with intentional flavors like horse blanket or cheerios or even "dank." But you don't make any of those beers anymore. It's all fruited sours now.

BRET: Our whole business plan has always been "Get Rich in Your Niche." Have a singular focus and own it. That focus used to be sour and wild beers. It used to be a little broader, but over time it's morphed into fruit. Our sole mindset is to be the best at making fruit beer.

MIKE: And it's a shame.

BRET: I wouldn't say that! But hearing you recount all these amazing beers we used to make, it makes me a little sad because I don't even know if I could brew them anymore. Do I even have the chops to brew a more traditional wild-style beer anymore? I don't know, but ultimately it doesn't matter. I'm so ingrained and loving what we're doing with fruit that, while I like remembering Clothesline, our original farmhouse beer, or Hearth, a dark farmhouse, I'm just glad it's put us on this track to living in fruit brewing paradise.

MIKE: I didn't have either of those, but I love a good saison. I don't think there's a better style beer in the world than a well-executed saison.

BRET: Same! But man, they just didn't sell. The first batch of saison we made when we first opened was still on tap nine months later.

MIKE: Why aren't you making Phrenology anymore? Why aren't you doing any wild yeast beers anymore? Are you a sellout? Are you over-fruiting everything because you're lazy? Defend yourself, man!

BRET: No one tells the wine maker that they're being lazy by making something just from fruit. That's the most over-fruited beverage you can get.

Actually, we're more akin to wine now with our fermentations than we are with beer. Even though it still takes an extreme level of talent as a brewer, as you chided, I think people thought we were selling out our original values. In a way, we did. But I don't think that's a bad thing or wrong. It's just different.

MIKE: At the end of the day, a business needs to stay in business. It's the primary goal of a business. Do you think that you could bring back a saison now and sell it with the reputation that Urban Artifact has built?

BRET: Nope. Americans just aren't going to buy wild or funky beers in the amount that we need to sell to be profitable.

MIKE: What made you think that this business model of sour beers was going to work? Nobody was doing it, but there's a lot of things that people don't do for a reason.

BRET: The sour beers that Scotty and I drank before opening Urban Artifact blew us away. I will always remember the first time we shared a bottle of Lindeman's Framboise. Tart, fruity and sweet. Three tastes I had no idea could exist in beer. That specific moment sparked an idea that began fermenting in my mind—of sour beer becoming a thing in the United States. The cultural changes occurring in the USA through the '90s around the explosion of sour candy. In fact, sour candy has only gained momentum over the last three decades. So, I began to think, if you like sour candy when you're younger, why aren't you going to like sour things when you're older? If you like sour candy when you're ten, why wouldn't you like sour beer when you're twenty-two or thirty-two or forty-two? I felt like there's opportunity here, a market gap waiting for sour beer. Historically speaking, Berliner weiss was the number one style of beer in the world at one point. It wasn't for a long period of time, but it was the most popular style of beer in the early 1800s. It was the original light beer. So, I thought, we can do this. We can bring sour beer back to global prominence.

MIKE: What are your biggest-selling beers now?

BRET: Our biggest-selling beer now is Gadget, which is blackberry and raspberry Midwest fruit tart, a style that we made up. Additionally, Peaches & Cream, which is a peach fruit tart with boatloads of vanilla served on nitro. Then, the strangest one of them all, Pickle.

MIKE: Yeah, let's talk about Pickle. Because while you cannot get a Cincinnati audience to buy a brilliant saison, they'll buy the shit out of a beer that tastes like pickle juice. Why was that even an idea? Let's start with that. How fucking high were you for that to sound like a good idea?

BRET: I love holiday beers. Great Lakes Christmas Ale is one of my all-time favorite beers. When we opened, I wanted to brew a bunch of different holiday beers and do a "Twelve Beers of Christmas" in the taproom. I didn't realize that you'd start running out of ideas pretty quickly when trying to stick to a tight theme like holiday beers. So, we learned about this old faux-German tradition of hiding a pickle in a Christmas tree.

MIKE: Oh my God, I like to hide my pickle places, but…

BRET: We put cucumbers, dill, coriander and salt into our gose [a sour German wheat beer], and just like that: Pickle Beer. The first year we made one keg, and it sold out quickly. People loved it, and we couldn't believe it.

A slurry of cucumbers fills the Urban Artifact brewery floor following some misadventures in brewing Pickle. *Courtesy of Urban Artifact.*

The next year we made a couple barrels, and it sold out again. The year after that, we brewed a large batch, and it sold out again. After a couple years of this, we decided, let's just make Pickle Beer all year.

MIKE: It makes me hate the American consumer, but good for you. It's interesting what people will latch on to and what they won't.

BRET: I guess familiarity is a large part of that. People know what pickles taste like, but they don't know what a horse blanket tastes like or even if that is supposed to be a good thing.

MIKE: Yeah, sadly. Like superhero movies. If you write a brilliant plot, it's a lot harder to sell that movie than if you make it the same stupid superhero movie as the rest. People will buy that ticket because they recognize it. It's predictable.

I started bringing my UC beer class here relatively early in Urban Artifact's existence. You and I started doing the tours for my class, and it's become tradition for me to end my class at Urban Artifact every semester. It's a good time, it's a good tour and you and I tend to throw back a couple pints. Early on, when I didn't really know you well, we were having some beers after the tour, and we started having a conversation about this new lager cellar that had been found in Over-the-Rhine. That happens periodically in Cincinnati. People find sealed-off lagering cellars. The crazy thing about this one was that there was an intact wood fermenter that had been sealed off in this basement for decades. Concurrently, somewhere in Russia, they'd uncovered mastodons that had been frozen for thousands of years. Some people studying them got smallpox, because the mastodons were still carrying live smallpox virus, even though they'd been frozen for thousands of years. Because you're a scientist and I'm not, this caused me to ask you if it was possible for yeast to live in that sealed-off cellar environment for eighty years or more. You said, "Sure, let's find out." We got a small team of brewers, a film crew, and we went searching for yeast.

BRET: We swabbed a bunch of different surfaces, gently scratching inside of this old fermenter, looking for a missing brewer's yeast. We took all those swabs and stuck them in a jar of wort and sealed it up to ferment and grow. We then waited six months before investigating what we had found.

MIKE: We sat down, and we tasted everything that had started to ferment—that wasn't black and that didn't smell absolutely vile. There were quite a few truly foul samples.

BRET: I remember one of those sample had the distinct aroma of filled baby diaper.

MIKE: And there was this lingering thought in my mind: Is this how you'd get smallpox from a mastodon? It's a little scary to drink jars of some bubbling foaming stuff when you don't really know why they're doing that.

BRET: I could see why you might have a little bit of trepidation around trying jars that look like they have strands of black alien fungus growing in them.

MIKE: Yeah, we probably could have died. Instead, one of those jars contained a live *Saccharomyces cerevisiae*—a brewer's yeast.

BRET: Despite all odds, we got one. One out of over a hundred and some samples, we got one.

MIKE: How shocked were you to find a brewer's yeast in that collection of stuff?

BRET: The entire time we were doing this, I was thinking to myself, "This will be fun because I get to go exploring under the city. I have an excuse to drink some beer in the middle of the day and crawl around in ancient tunnels. I'm going to learn something, even if we find nothing." And I was convinced we would find nothing. After you sprung the plan on me that you were going to bring a film crew, I'm thinking to myself, "Oh my God, little does Mike and crew know, but we're most certainly not going to find anything." We're wasting these guys' time. It's literally trying to find a needle in a haystack, blindfolded. But we found a unique lost-to-time brewer's yeast that we named Missing Linck, in honor of the F.&J.A. Linck Brewery that once stood above these now defunct cellars. Later that year, we ceremoniously gave the yeast to the city. It's banked at Omega Yeast Labs in Chicago, and brewers can now brew their own modern beers with it.

Jordan Wakeman and Josh Elliott bathe Olive, a formerly homeless cat with a rags-to-riches story. Olive was a hardworking brewery cat before being forced into early retirement by the Ohio Department of Agriculture. She now lives the lazy life with brewer Jordan Wakeman. *Courtesy of Urban Artifact.*

MIKE: It also led to us doing the Missing Linck Festival. The first time we brewed that yeast strain for public consumption was back in 2019, at the original Missing Linck Fest.

BRET: It is a lot of fun to brew with that yeast. After five years now of playing around with that yeast and brewing different beers with it, I still don't fully understand all the different expressions of flavor it can create. Which is such a fun thing to continue to figure out as a brewer.

MIKE: It's been a blast to turn what should have been a nothing burger into a festival around a yeast that we donated to the city on a day that the city now recognizes as Missing Linck Day, every June 1. It has the hallmarks of one of the old-school beer festivals.

BRET: It's been so amazing to see how much people get excited about the story of Missing Linck. To be able to taste Cincinnati history in beer form is so fun and uniquely Cincinnati. It's not what I imagined at all when we first started this cellar-dwelling adventure, but I love being able to share this beer history—and the response from the homebrewers has been fantastic. To see what they're brewing with this yeast has been an honor. Some of my favorite beers this city has ever produced have come out of the Missing Linck Homebrew Competition.

MIKE: We've been lucky that Roxanne Westendorf, a past president of the local homebrew club the Bloatarians, has taken over the organization of the homebrew competition. She has a storied history with homebrewing and the American Homebrewers Association. She made a great point to me recently about why this competition is different from the rest. Usually, commercial brewers hate it when a homebrewer tries to tell them how to make beer, but this yeast is so new and so weird that the homebrewers are having conversations about it on an equal footing. They're learning together. That's reminiscent of the early days of craft beer, when Charlie Papazian and Ken Grossman would make a beer together in somebody's kitchen, then go out and change the world.

BRET: Absolutely. Because homebrewers can afford to experiment and make mistakes on a small scale, they actually have as much knowledge about using this yeast as commercial brewers do, because they can't afford to throw batches out. It does feel like we're bringing back a little spirit of the pioneer craft days.

EPILOGUE(S)

Bret Kollmann Baker: Just Don't Do It

Do not start a brewery. Don't do it. You won't like it. Glorified janitor, paper pusher, bean counter, human resources hijinks, babysitter, alcoholic, keg jockey, plumber, mechanic, electrician, architect, boiler repairman, control panel programmer, MS paint label creator, jury- and jerry-rigger, yeast farmer, wort wrangler and, most of all, *sellout*! These are your jobs as a brewery owner. Things you are not: Master Brewer, Recipe Maestro, Steve Jobs, any successful brewer from eras past, Clever Punny Beer Name Writer, Well Paid and, most certainly you are *not in control*.

"But, Bret," you say emphatically, "I am going to brew what I want, and people will respond to that! I will brew it and they will come."

If only that were true! There once was an era when that could happen, when craft beer was nascent and everything was exciting, glittery and fresh. People were exploring their options, and for the most part, craft beer was good. Choices, while expanding, were still limited, and preferences were not yet fully developed by the consumer. The brewer ran wild and brewed exactly what they wanted, and it usually sold well enough to keep the lights on and the kettle roiling. Craft beer was growing in leaps and bounds. But what we failed to see at the time was that consumers' have preferences, and their choices matter. The customer is always right in matters of taste. Over time, through financial trials and tribulations, "We brew what we want" took a hard, 180-degree turn into "We brew what sells." Are you willing to bend the knee to capitalism? Or will you hold strong to your vision and values as a brewery owner? When your distributor is knocking on the brewery door and telling you to make another IPA over your brilliantly sublime dark lager, will you cave to their demands? How will you respond the 238th time a beer buyer at a bar tells you they don't want your perfectly brewed Belgian triple and, instead, asks what new IPAs you have? Is your constitution—more importantly, your wallet—deep enough to handle the constant style dredging?

Beer recipes are not sacrosanct. There is no Coca-Cola–style secret recipe when it comes to beer. Don't get me wrong, there is artificially created marketing mystique surrounding certain brands. Guinness is the pinnacle example, but that's nothing more than masterful advertising gimmickry. Any brewer worth their salt can make a damn good Guinness clone, and if you cannot, then you best be prepared to spend the money on a head brewer who can. The opposite is, of course, also true. "I got this," you say assuredly to your investors. "I am the premier brewer in my state!" Maybe, but are you also the premier marketer and salesperson in your state? Because you can't have a brewery without sales. Brewing is the easy part.

Are you ready to make no money, possibly ever? Are you ready to put your house on the line to secure that SBA loan? Bankruptcy cannot save your house from the federal government on a small business loan. They will take everything from you. Can your partner tolerate you when you're stressed all the time? What about the rest of your family? Do you have kids? Can your partner willingly carry an oversized load of child rearing duties while you tend to your newest child, the brewery? It took us more than three years at Urban Artifact before my business partners, Scott and Scotty, and I were able to pay ourselves a minimum-wage salary. Scotty lived with my wife and I for more than three years just to financially survive. There was even a time when we sold our house, and all three of us lived with my in-laws. Can you imagine living with your business partner, your wife and your in-laws, all under the in-laws' roof!? Thank goodness my wife has the patience, strength and understanding of a biblical angel. Otherwise, none of our relationships would have survived the emotional hardships.

What is your endgame? Sell out to a large-scale brewery like Miller? Well, guess what? They ain't buying. Small-scale manufacturing in the United States of America died decades ago for a reason. Manufacturing is hard manual labor, and running a brewery isn't a party. Sure, you can neck a few pints after work at the bar on the company's dime, but do you really want to be drinking every single day? Do you have the mental fortitude to show up in the taproom, with a smile on your face, to chat up customers after twelve hours of busting ass and sweating in the brewhouse all day? Are you prepared for the physical and mental toll from being expected to share beers at every single meeting that occurs after noon? There are days I look in the mirror, and all I can see is Slurms, the party worm, from *Futurama*. I'm so tired of "partying." So very tired.

If you can answer all these questions thoughtfully and your dream of opening a brewery still remains all consuming, then congratulations: you're one of us. One of the stubborn, the eternally poor, the rubber boot–wearing wretched, the physically exhausted, the emotionally drained and stretched thinner with more stress damage than a plate of your grandma's finest bone china. You're one of the few who can wrangle the worst of hangovers and still show up at 6:00 a.m. to mash-in. You probably won't get any benefits from your Icarus-like assault on the sun, except for maybe one: the pure and simple joy of seeing a total stranger savor a pint of your beer and watch them enjoy it! Cheers, you filthy animal. You're one of us. Good luck with your poor choices, and I'll see you in the taproom.

Michael D. Morgan: Not Dead Yet

Among activities usually conducted with your clothes on, there's nothing that I'd rather do than write, which is how I got talked into another damn beer book. I never saw writing as a viable career path, though, so I followed other, meandering, often arbitrary routes to financial survival. After four years at Ohio University seeking a BA degree, I woke up late one morning with a hangover lying on the floor of my apartment in Athens, Ohio. The sound of the landlord's maintenance people coming in the front door downstairs roused me to consciousness. I was supposed to be out of there already, and I didn't want to be confronted with that fact or the filthy state of the place, so I crawled out the bedroom window onto a jutting first-floor roof, jumped into a tree, shimmied down, got into the car packed with all my stuff and left town. I was six credit hours short of graduating. My mom wasn't impressed. She suggested a job in the tobacco fields, hoping that I'd learn the value of a college degree—or at least the cost of not having one. I got a bartending job instead, which I overlaid with construction laborer, substitute teacher, traveling collection agent for a telemarketing company, followed by pilot car

Bret and Mike display feats of strength during a Missing Linck Fest tour in 2023. *Courtesy of Urban Artifact.*

driver for oversize semi-truck loads. Eventually, I conceded that mom was right. I needed a grown-up job.

I went back to OU for a summer semester to graduate and then turned to the last refuge of a skilled bullshit artist with no proficiency in either math or science: I became an attorney. After a few years of being a sole practitioner, I found myself asking, "Who the fuck wants to spend their life being a lawyer?" I still don't have a complete answer to that question, but I figured out as much of it as I needed to: not me. I briefly got into political campaigns, started selling real estate, and I ran a few nonprofits. That's when I started using beer history and craft beer events as a tool of historic preservation and neighborhood revitalization. Beer was a means to an end. I didn't know anything about beer history at first, but I could read and I'm a diligent researcher. I didn't know anything about special events either, but my misspent youth gave me a natural affinity for throwing edgy parties. In addition to Bockfest, I ran the first, big craft beer tappings for Christian Moerlein; conceived of, licensed and built the Bier Garten at Findlay Market; and created the first brewery heritage tours, along with a lot of smaller debauches that all hazily merge in images that feel like someone else's life.

Later, I stopped drinking for health reasons. I started feeling amazing in the mornings, hiking a lot more, losing weight, working out and becoming astoundingly productive, and for the first time in my life I learned that I could drive somewhere for the evening and not worry about how to get home without being arrested. Who knew that was a thing? It was great, albeit a little boring at times. Then I was asked if I would teach a beer history and appreciation class at the University of Cincinnati. Well, shit! I'm like the Michael Corleone of beer. It isn't writing, but I really enjoy teaching. Over the years, I've taught everything from kindergarten to paralegal classes at crooked for-profit degree mills, and I've always coveted a position at a legitimate college. More importantly, I was told that "getting my foot in the door" could lead to teaching other subjects, possibly becoming a full-time professor. So, I started teaching beer history and helping undergraduates transition from Natural Light to good beer, doing tastings, leading tours to breweries and, of course, drinking again. Almost a decade later of teaching two sections of "Hops & History: Introduction to Beer" every semester, I now teach an additional beer class focusing on the history and broader social implications of the craft beer movement. I've overseen the creation of a brewing industry certificate program, and I've been tasked with studying the feasibility of opening a University of Cincinnati brewery. That's all good,

Mike during the filming of the documentary *Wild Yeast and the Missing Linck*, chronicling the discovery of the pre-Prohibition brewing yeast strain that is used during Missing Linck Festival, the first Saturday in June. This project sparked all subsequent *Brew Skies* productions. *Courtesy of Urban Artifact.*

roles that I'm appreciate of, but the best part for me is that it finally might lead to becoming a real, honest-to-God professor who teaches classes that don't have anything to do with beer.

The point is that I'm not "Beer Dave." I didn't set out with the intent of making a career in brewing-adjacent fields. I fell into it and then went with the flow. I'm not complaining. It wasn't the life I planned, but almost nothing about my life looks anything like what I expected it to at the age when I crouched behind a shed and drank my first beer. I'm a thousand miles away from my financial goals, starting to watch some of my most successful Gen X friends plan for retirement while I'm still trying to figure out what I'm going to be when I grow up. But I do get paid to do a lot of ridiculous things that people sitting in cubicles daydream about getting paid for. So, there's that.

What I enjoy about teaching beer classes, co-hosting *Brew Skies Happy Hour* podcast and *Brew Skies Barstool Perspective* with Bret, as well as writing about beer, is the rich tapestry of context surrounding the beverage. Historically, some anthropologists believe that beer is the primary reason that we stopped living solely as hunter-gatherers and started farming grain crops. One of the few things that we know about the lost colony of Roanoke is that the colonists brewed. A shortage of beer is why the *Mayflower* landed at Plymouth Rock. It saved lives during cholera epidemics. It was at the root of riots and ethnic divisions. Beer's association with the German enemy during World War I gave us Prohibition, and then it became as American as apple die during World War II. In the modern social context, craft brewing is the one, single industry since Reagan was elected president in which small businesses have collectively posed a threat to the market share of huge, multinational behemoths. Beer is more than a commodity. It is evolution, survival, warfare and friendship, and it's often at the core of neighborhood revitalization. People enter different aspects of the beer business for a variety of reasons, but the ones who do it purely for money almost always realize that there are much easier ways to build wealth. The ones who stick around, whether they struggle or thrive, all have an ulterior drive. Whether they're motivated by a respect for history and tradition, a love of science or they just have a stubborn rebellious streak, there's something a little bit weird about most of them, something that sets them apart from the pack. That's why I enjoy talking to them, and it's why I hope I'm fortunate enough to keep having these conversations for a long time to come.

ABOUT THE AUTHOR(S)

BRET KOLLMANN BAKER has a BS in chemical engineering and a degree in brewing science and is one of the co-owners of Urban Artifact, America's largest fruit brewery. He's also the United States Brewery Ambassador for Les Vergers Boiron (a French fruit puree company). At home, Bret is married to his wonderful wife, Stephanie, with whom he raises their chaotic good–aligned daughter, Joanna.

MICHAEL D. MORGAN teaches beer and planning courses at the University of Cincinnati. He's also a notorious provocateur and the author of *Over-the-Rhine: When Beer Was King* (2010) and *Cincinnati Beer* (2019), among other things. He continues to live in exile in Newport with Amy and two criminals named Julie Ann and Rickie.

Together, Baker and Morgan cohost the *Brew Skies Happy Hour* podcast, an extensive, ongoing history of American craft beer that includes interviews with all the legendary pioneers of the industry. They also host *Brew Skies Barstool Perspective*, a YouTube show where they provide a weekly recap of news from the alcoholic beverage industry, along with a lot of ridiculous and periodically offensive commentary.